Inspiring Stories For Healing From Trauma

OVERCOMING
HEART BLOCKS

REGELINE EDEN SABBAT

OVERCOMING HEART BLOCKS

Orders by U.S. trade bookstores and wholesalers.
Email info@ BeyondPublishing.net

The Beyond Publishing Speakers Bureau can bring authors to your live event. For more information or to book an event contact the Beyond Publishing Speakers Bureau speak@BeyondPublishing.net

The Author can be reached directly at BeyondPublishing.net

Manufactured and printed in the United States of America distributed globally by BeyondPublishing.net

New York | Los Angeles | London | Sydney

ISBN: 978-1-637921-96-8

TABLE OF CONTENTS

FOREWORD

by Tanya Gold, MD

I've known Gigi for sometime now. She's the author of several awesome books, has an amazing podcast called "walk with me" and is a wonderful public speaker. She's had a hard life, that's an understatement, but she's managed to overcome so much.

Finding the Lord, she's used her beautiful gifts of sharing her powerful story and helping others navigate their emotional heart blocks. She is truly a gifted leader and a blessing in this world.

The messages in this book magnifies the importance of getting help in finding your path to healing.It's not over after a tragedy. It's just the beginning, New opportunity for growth and planting the seeds to be your best authentic self. We've all been through something and have a story. The powerful message here is to "never give up". You are a child of G-d and here for a reason. Believe in yourself "Step Up". Bring in joy and blessings in your life because it matters. it's not what you get in life but what you give. And I thank Gigi for giving so much of herself. 😁🖤

Tanya Gold MD, author of 7 habits of extremely happy people

Many people develop a heart block after a traumatic experience.

Heart Blocks are blocks around your heart that have developed as a result of trauma, and they interfere with one's ability to live a fulfilling life.

Overcoming Heart Blocks helps people overcome their Heart blocks and heal from trauma.

This book includes stories from incredible people who have overcome their heart blocks, and each heart block survivor provides helpful information and action steps for you to begin to transform your life.

CHAPTER 1

Heart Blocks Intertwine with Trauma

Regeline Sabbat Also Known As Gigi

We are not born into this world with a heart block. A heart block is developed from a traumatic event/experience. How do I know this? It is because I had developed my own heart block at the age of eight years old after I was sexually assaulted by two individuals. This traumatic event/experience changed the trajectory of my entire life.

After, I was sexually assaulted, it affected my social relationships and my trust in others. And, for so many years I wondered why. However, it wasn't until after I was sexually assaulted again as an adult, that I figured out why. I realized it is because of the heart block I had developed due to trauma.

Immediately after being sexually assaulted as an adult, I'll never forget waking up the next morning, because I woke up feeling numb to pain. I was in shock and all I could think about was how did this happen again, because I literally took all the precautions to avoid being sexually assaulted again. However, I had to acknowledge the reality, that this happened again, and I realized I had been here before, and God got me through then and he could do it again.

My faith brought me through the toughest challenges in my life, and your faith and keeping God first in your life can help you overcome the challenges in your life as well. Never give up.

Keep God first in your life and watch your life transform. God wants to be a part of all areas of our lives, and he does not want us to fight our battles/challenges alone. Give your battles/challenges to God.

Fill in the blank

Do you have a heart block?

____

____

____

____

____

How did you develop your heart block?

____

____

____

____

____

No matter what Trauma you have faced in your life you too can overcome the heart blocks you have developed, with God First.

God will heal your heart block, but you need to Let God In

If you are experiencing a heart block right now. Take a moment right now and pray.

Ask God to heal your heart block.

Let go of your battle with your Heart Block and let God take care of this battle for you

Fill in the blank

Explain how you feel after giving your battle/challenge with your heart block to God to help you?

____

____

____

____

____

____

____

____

____

____

____

____

I truly believe every individual who has developed a heart block can overcome their heart block.

How do I know this?

This book includes inspiring stories of individuals who have had heart blocks in their lives. If they can overcome their heart blocks, you can to.

My dream is that each of you who have a heart block can overcome your heart blocks, so you can live Gods purpose for your life.

Every one's story is unique. As you read the following chapters pay attention to how each individual developed their heart block and how they overcame their heart block.

Each story truly has helpful information to help you heal from Trauma. Healing is a process, and by you taking the time to read this book and each chapter I am proud of you.

You may be in fear and not know what is on the other side of overcoming your heart block, but please be assured that God will not bring you to anything he won't get you through. Therefore, it is not by accident you have this book in your hand. You can and you will overcome your heart block. I believe in you. Now, I just need you to believe in yourself as well and remember with God all things are possible. Keep the faith. Faith is believing in the things you can not see.

I'll see you on the other side of your heart block, which is overcoming.......

REGELINE SABBAT

also known as Gigi

Regeline Sabbat also known as Gigi, is the CEO and Founder of Life Service Center of America, LLC, Motivational Keynote Speaker, 3x Best Selling Author of the " Walk With Me" and " God First" books that have been endorsed by Les Brown. Gigi is also the Co-Author for several best selling book collaborations, and she is a Life Coach and Confidence Coach. First generation Haitian American, Financial Expert, Florida Chapter Leader for World Women Conference & Awards, the host of Walk With Me Podcast on JRQTV, Domestic Violence Advocate, Sexual Assault Advocate, Breast Cancer Advocate, Human Trafficking Advocate, and Mental Health Advocate, etc. She is an experienced leader who has adopted a traditional approach to help people grow spiritually, financially, professionally and/or personally. She does this by setting clear and measurable goals for those that are ready to take action and experience life growth and transformation. She also helps people get unstuck financially.

As far as focusing and transformation goes, Regeline truly believes multi-skilled individuals make great leaders. It's not about focusing on so many things at once, but it is about utilizing all of your skills for the greater good and overall fulfilling God's purpose for our lives and to serve his people.

https://allmylinks.com/gigisabbat

CHAPTER 2

Take control of your Heart Blocks! Remove all stressors in your life

Guerline Sabbat

Over 25 years ago, I was working in the Intensive Care Unit, and I started feeling very strange, so I asked the nurses to put me on a cardiac monitor because my heart was racing it felt like my heart was coming out of my mouth and felt like I was going to die. My heart was beating 180 times per minute. They immediately took me to the Emergency room and they later admitted me to the ICU unit that I worked. They gave me a lot of different cardiac drugs and they finally decided to do a cardiac catheterization. It was negative. All others tests and lab work were negative. They put me on a beta blocker while I was in the hospital and when I got home I decided that I was going to wean myself off because I felt like I was stressed, 3 babies, working full time plus a lot of overtime.

As a nurse I always think that I can save every patient. I was a hard worker and basically I never stopped. I was over performing in every area in my life: work, mother, family, wife. I used to work 140-150 hours every 2 weeks. We started building our retirement home just at 30 years. I started to realize that I was doing it to myself. I took a month off from work. Money or no money I did not care because I was determined not to become dependent of that medication. I felt like I was too young to die. So I completely stop the beta blocker within 2 weeks , my husband took my family and I on a vacation and by the time I came back home, I felt like I was healed. I never had anymore episodes for 15 years because I learned to remove the stressors of my life.

Ten years ago I was working as a Director of Nursing and 1 of the doctors was very abusive toward the nurses. I requested a meeting with him, the CEO, and the chief of nursing and I let him him know then that his behavior is unacceptable and that I was not going to support that. He agreed to work on it. The next morning he came to my office and told me that he can do whatever he wants, and I gave him a good piece of my mind. Two hours later I ended in The Emergency Room again with the same rapid heart rate. My daughter was in the hospital with me but I never told her what happened. Again all the cardiac tests were negative.

When I left the hospital this time I decided to take control of my heart . That was the last time I had a heart block. Take control of yourself and your emotions. Don't let no one push you to the limit. Remove all stressors in your life.

GUERLINE SABBAT

Registered Nurse

CHAPTER 3

Unblocked and Unstoppable

Dr. Mary Kaye Holmes

What happens when the heart is blocked? What happens when the very essence of who you are becomes hindered, suffocated, gridlocked, and imprisoned? What happens when you lose your sense of self through trauma and you feel as if you'll never recover? The result is a loss of self-esteem and a silencing of your voice. I developed a heart block when I was just a teenager, trapped inside a small one-bedroom apartment that belonged to my trafficker. I recall feeling as if the walls were constantly closing in around me. Every day, I hoped I could conjure the courage to stand up to this man who was 21 years my senior, but each time I cowered back in fear. Ashamed of what I perceived to be a self-imposed prison, I blamed myself for being controlled and manipulated. My heart was so blocked I shrank down to a soft-spoken shell of a girl who desperately yearned to be free. Freedom was always so close, but yet so far, because I didn't think anyone cared and I didn't want to leave my current prison in exchange for the prison of poverty. If I went back to my mother's house, what was waiting for me? Section 8? Food stamps? Struggle? Ridicule? I felt trapped. I felt stuck. I felt boxed in because my heart was blocked.

My heart was blocked by low self-esteem. Had I valued myself and saw myself worthy of being free, I could have defied my trafficker's orders and escaped on many occasions. When I was told not to use the phone nor leave the apartment building, I felt paralyzed by the fear of the unknown. I didn't know what he would do to me if I were caught. I didn't know how bad he would beat me. Sometimes, it wasn't about the physical abuse, but the emotional abuse. How bad would he make me feel about myself? The emotional abuse and manipulation were the most effective because I believed I was worthless and no one else would want me. I believed I couldn't make it on my own and my only recourse was to turn back to a poverty-stricken environment. I even believed this was a form of love, because after a while I confused control with concern and extreme restrictions with protection. When your heart is blocked, every embrace, no matter how sinister, can feel like acceptance.

My self-esteem was broken down to the point where I perceived myself as a worthless human being, an inconvenience taking up valuable space in a world. It took seven years for me to escape my trafficker, but it took nearly twenty years for me to recover. Along the way, I watched other young women grow up and into their own. I watched them become take-charge women, conquering one goal after the next. I watched them graduate from college, get married, start lucrative careers, and raise healthy families. I watched them flourish while I floundered. I watched them soar while I sank deeper and deeper into depression. But, one day, I decided to turn my envy into admiration. No longer, would I stand by and watch from the sidelines simply waiting my turn. I learned that success leaves clues and I studied the patterns of my predecessors.

However, while my self-esteem was slowly but surely rising, I had to get over one more hurdle. I had to find my voice. For years, I allowed others to speak for me and I shuddered at the thought of raising my voice and being seen. My doctor even diagnosed me with social anxiety disorder. Being around other people caused extreme nervousness, fear of embarrassment, and a constant worry about how others saw me. I was afraid to be me. So afraid, in fact, that I would shake uncontrollably, sweat profusely, clench my teeth, and keep my eyes toward the ground. The last thing I wanted to do was be heard. Because of the heart block, my voice has become silenced.

The greatest book ever written quotes Jesus as saying, "Out of the abundance of the heart, the mouth speaks." Truer words have never been spoken, because what's in the heart of man will certainly come out of his mouth. Not only that, but the Bible also teaches that "as a man thinks in his heart, so is he." Consider this: what happens to the person whose heart is blocked? If the heart is blocked, abundance cannot come forth. As a result, the mouth does not speak and therefore the voice is silent. If the heart is blocked, no matter what the person thinks in his heart, they can't truly become all they are destined to be. That was my story. My heart was blocked from the trauma of being human trafficked and as a result, I had no voice and I had no clue who I was or where I was going. I was utterly lost.

After years of control and manipulation, I wasn't used to making my own choices. I was never completely sure of what I truly liked or disliked. How did I want to dress or wear my hair? How did I want to walk or talk? What did I want to do for a living? Where did I want to live? All of these questions, and more, bombarded my mind on a daily basis. As a result, I constantly changed my hair color and hair styles. In fact, I changed my hair styles so much that I became known for wearing a different wig every day. I bounced from one job to another. For instance, I was a home health aide, a pharmacy technician, a customer service representative, a collections agent, a telemarketer, a chiropractor's assistant, data entry clerk, a hotel manager, a paralegal, a freelance writer, just to name a few! I changed career paths more times than I could count, and my hopes ranged from being a registered nurse to an auto mechanic and everything in between. As if that weren't bad enough, I moved nine times in 10 years, each time unknowingly uprooting my two children and creating a life of instability. I didn't know who I was or where I was going. All I knew was that I was chasing freedom.

Thankfully, I found freedom when I found my voice. One day, I decided to own my story and take all the trauma and turn it into a testimony. The moment I took authority over my truth, I realized who I was and who I was not. I realized that I am not what happened to me. I realized that I am no longer a victim. I am freedom fighter. I am a survivor. I am more than a conqueror. I am a warrior. I am resilient. I am a rescuer. With every realization my heart opened up. My heart opened up and made room for love, trust, and forgiveness. My heart opened up and made room for peace, faith, and freedom. My heart opened up and compassion poured out. With that compassion I spread awareness about human trafficking in the effort to rescue others. With that same compassion I am committed to helping others find their freedom within themselves.

I learned that there was more to just surviving trauma – you can actually THRIVE beyond trauma! When I finished my bachelor's degree and made the decision to apply to law school, I was nearly paralyzed by indecision and uncertainty. How can you speak up for anyone else when you're afraid to speak up for yourself? You're a fraud and everyone will see it. This was just one of the many thoughts that entered my mind. However, I overcame the haunting visuals of me making a fool of myself in a courtroom in front of a room filled with judging eyes, and I pushed past the fear and pursued my law school career anyway. Today I serve as in-house counsel to a prestigious insurance and investments firm. The young girl trapped in that one-bedroom apartment couldn't see that there was a lawyer inside of her. She couldn't see the best-selling author, the international motivational speaker, or the life coach. Now, beyond the heart block, I see her. I see me! There was more to me than what met the eye and there is more to you as well.

You, too, can access your own power and become empowered to transition out of trauma. You, too, can unblock your heart and unlock your mind through the sharing of your own story and discovering your true purpose. It takes self-discovery and self-acceptance. When you discover who you truly are, embrace it. When you discover that everything that has happened didn't happen to you, but for you, you walk in power. Take what happened, put it under your feet, stand on it, and take control over it – now your pain becomes a platform that lifts you up. Trauma may have blocked your heart, but the truth will make you free. Stand in your truth, stand on your truth, and you will never be stopped!

DR. MARY KAYE HOLMES

Dr. Mary Kaye Holmes is a #1 international best-selling author and author of ten books including her most recent best-selling memoir, "Trapped in Plain Sight: The Unfamiliar Face of Human Trafficking." She is also a speaker, Certified Life & Success Coach, award-winning founder of the global movement "Outlive the Labels", and a mouthpiece for criminal justice reform and human trafficking awareness. As a 2x survivor of human trafficking, domestic violence and incarceration, she is a sought-after trusted authority on thriving beyond adversity and speaks from her heart concerning real issues that plague women from all walks of life.

Dr. Mary Kaye's latest endeavor is her 501(c)3, the H.A.L.O.

Campaign which creates pathways to employment and entrepreneurship for human trafficking survivors. In addition, she is the co-founder of the non-profit Waterbury Community Action Network, Inc. and is the executive pastor at Triumph Christian Center of Waterbury, CT.

Dr. Mary Kaye is a graduate of New York Law School and currently serves as In-House Corporate Counsel for a NYC investment and insurance firm. Her greatest accomplishment is being the mother of her two sons and being married to the love of her life, Terry.

CHAPTER 4

A Message of Hope

Dr. Saf Buxy

Anecdotal experiences are, of course, respective, yet I am a firm believer that a lesson lived is a lesson learned. Through the tumultuousness of my life, I have ascertained a certain comprehension of trauma, adoption, mental health and addiction which cannot be taught or read; thus, this conceivably gives me the authority to share my experience in the hope of helping others.

In 1972, I was born 6 weeks premature and adopted at birth or as I now call it relinquished at birth. There's no relinquishment without trauma/there is no adoption without trauma. It's about the grief of a baby who has been waiting up to nine months to meet somebody who they're not going to meet. And in the womb how we're set up to bond. Instead, I was abandoned and entered into a family where I didn't genetically fit with an impossible job description, the job description of having to be somebody that I could never actually be to fix a wound

In 1983, I had my first drink, a bottle of vodka neat. I was 11 years old. Subsequently, I was unconscious for over 9 hours and had my first of 2 stomach pumps. This was the start of a 33 year addiction. An addiction that has caused pain, destruction, chaos and a lot of mayhem.

Addiction does not discriminate and it comes in many forms. Many people have the preconceived impression of an addict to be an unaspiring and apathetic person, maybe someone with pitiable hygiene whose life solely revolves around their addiction. Whilst I can subscribe to the thought, that addiction is debilitating and at times all-consuming, the stereotype of what an addict is should be dispelled. I was born into a very dysfunctional family but was adopted at birth by a wonderful middle-class couple, attended an acclaimed boarding school and grew up to be a loving husband and father. Despite my ostensibly picture-perfect life, I became ensnared by the power of addiction which caused havoc in my life and affected my loved ones to a great degree. Alcohol, Cannabis, Cocaine, Crystal Meth and gambling were my main vices.

I was a abused physically, racially, verbally and sexually for 6 years of my life on a daily basis from the age of 11. I suffered wounding bereavements, developed an inferiority complex from a very early age. I was diagnosed as bipolar. To be frank, I don't know if these events caused my addiction or if it was some sort of predisposition, but I do know that I am an addict and will always be an addict of some sort. It may sound counter-intuitive to some that I use the term addict in the present tense when my aim is to help people change their lives, but for me it all comes down to accepting. Acceptance is the answer to all of my problems today. It was unnerving for me to ask for help, but in all honesty, it was scarier to continue to do what I was doing. My destructive behavior and volatile mental health that addiction caused plagued my life to becoming unmanageable, but a person may have to hit rock-bottom or in my case just be completely done in order to value their existence. I vehemently believe that the potency of my self-destruction led me to recovery. I find it difficult to verbalize the extent of the perils of addiction, or the 'madness' as I call it. Primarily because addiction often causes a loss of inhibition and rational thought; I used to act uncharacteristically, sometimes delving into the realm of the unethical. I was attracted to the gangster lifestyle and everything that came with it.

Being around people throughout my life especially when I was a vulnerable 11 year old, I was beaten daily, humiliated daily, abused sexually, I was regularly told that I looked like fat brown Terrorist, being told I was ugly, being told I was stupid. However, I quickly realized based on the energy that, that was not okay. Those experiences along with thousands that I could name created, not only this wall, but a belief in my own brokenness. So I walked around from age 11 , feeling disconnected, feeling broken, feeling like there was something very wrong with me, and with the world. And soon after, I found relief from that. It came in the form of drugs and alcohol. As a matter of fact, the moment I drank that bottle of vodka for the first time, had that line of cocaine and piped some crystal meth I felt alive again. it brought relief from that psychic pain that I was in, it brought relief from me carrying around these core beliefs of my own unworthiness. So, I have come to recognize that drugs and alcohol are not the problem. They're actually a solution. In my own life, they were a solution to my belief in my own brokenness. Now, I'm not just talking about a belief in my mind, I had cemented, the energy of brokenness, that I am not lovable, I'm not good enough, I am not worthy and I carried these core false beliefs around for many years. And I found relief from alcohol and drugs. So, by the time I turned 43, I did come into recovery. And that began my journey of returning to the essential truth of who and what I am.

So if we come into the world as this whole and perfect being, and we're taught anything that's counter to that, that could be considered a traumatic experience. And so of course, if we feel broken or damaged internally, we begin to look to the world to try to feel whole again. That might be the simplest or the broadest definition of addiction, looking for someone, something or some behaviour outside of ourselves to try to heal or fix something that feels broken within. So, if we look at the addicted self through this broader lens, we can recognize that we do have physical, intellectual, emotional, and spiritual aspects to what created our addictive tendencies. We do recognize that spiritually, underneath all of that there is still a whole perfect spiritual being, and that through different cultural experiences or influences, we start to believe in and even more importantly, experience ourselves as broken in some way. And as I said before, if we feel broken internally, we begin to look to the world to try to feel whole again just like I did.

Anything that happens in our life, other than something that confirms the greater reality that we are whole and perfect, is actually traumatic. And in that way, we cannot only begin to normalize trauma as an experience of being human. But even more importantly, we can move beyond comparing our trauma or our sense of trauma to another person.

Even if we don't have a memory of the trauma, we still have the experience of the traumatic event. And again, it's not so much what happened. It's more about what we experienced about what happened. That creates the trauma wound.

So how did I overcome my heart blocks?

By breaking the fantasy of living in a one-sided world-If you're looking for happiness without sadness, health without disease, pleasure without pain and more, then you're living in the lowest level of your animal brain, the amygdala-you're looking for a dopamine fix. You're being sold the fantasy that there is positive without negative. The more you strive for a one-sided world looking for the fantasy, the more your life becomes a nightmare, because you're striving for something that is not available, and trying to avoid something that is unavoidable. In Buddhism they used to say that desiring something that is not available and avoiding something that is not avoidable is a source of human suffering. When you live by your highest values you embrace pleasure in pain. When you live by your highest values you embrace support and challenge equally. But when you're living in your animal nature;

your lower values, off you go towards a one-sided world. If you want to be a master, you have to live by your highest values and wake up your executive centre that has reason and embrace both sides of life objectively, or otherwise you'll be vulnerable to the animal's behavior, and you'll be sold the fantasy searching for the unavailable and trying to avoid the unavoidable. Anytime you get addicted to a fantasy you create a nightmare out of your life.

We are all living by a set of priorities. Things that are most important to least important, highest priority to lowest priority, highest value to lower values. A hierarchy that whenever there is setting a goal, or intention or an objective that is aligned with the highest value, or at least higher values, we tend to be disciplined, reliable and focus our perseverance, hence, we tend to not let anything outside stop us. Recognizing this, I found that I could see whatever challenges I had, as feedback to refine and keep achieving, and I was achieving it by waking up my natural leadership capacities. This undoubtedly gave me a greater self-worth. But if we attempt to do something that are low on our values, the values become more extrinsic and require motivation to keep us focused on it. So, if you are doing something low on your values, you'll procrastinate, hesitate and become frustrated unless somebody gives you a reward to do it or a punishment if you don't do it. And if you require some extrinsic motivation to get you to do something, you are off track for who you are, because your highest value is where your identity and your true authentic self is expressed. So, off the back of my trauma and consequent heart blocks I often felt that people were smarter than me, more successful than me, had more wealth than me, more stable relationships than me, were more socially savvy than me, were more physically fit and more spiritually aware than me, hence I would compare myself to them. It's very possible that I injected some of their values and tried to imitate them in some way into my life. This was not my values. Whenever you set a goal that's not really truly meaningful and most important to you and your highest values, you'll automatically decrease the probability of achieving it. You will not have focus, and in turn you will procrastinate and rely on outside motivation to keep you focused on it. You will often find yourself giving up, and you feel like a failure and self- depreciate. All of these things that you think are self-sabotage are actually feedback mechanisms to make sure you're setting true objectives that are aligned with your true values, not fantasies that aren't you, or a one sided positive thinking all the time. When you have the idea of setting a real objective that you can obtain you don't have self-sabotage. Instead, you have self-discipline. It's actually your psyche and your experiences, trying to get you to be the most authentic, empowered and most inspired you.

If you want to be accountable, and you want to be organized in your life, understand there's two sides to everything. If you ground yourself and embrace the two sides of life, you won't set fantasies and create nightmares, you'll be empowered and you'll do something amazing with Planet Earth, and that is amazing and is real transformation. You have always a balance in life.

The Buxy Recovery Process that I created comes in Five parts:

the root cause

breaking the cycle

a return to wholeness

living in your highest priority values

application of omnipresent laws

DR. SAF BUXY

Dr. Saf Buxy is a Social Behavioral Mentor and Addiction Psychotherapist. He is an Author, Speaker, TV, Radio and Social Media personality, and respected pioneer in Addiction Consulting. He delivers life-changing material and personal expertise to shift clients towards a more fulfilling future.

Through gaining personal empirical knowledge, Dr. Saf Buxy incorporates this experience along with research, training, and vocation in guiding those afflicted by trauma and addiction. The complexity of human behavior requires a non-prescriptive approach; Dr. Saf transforms people's lives through mentally disbanding the cause of their pain.

As a proponent of breaking free from 'the madness', Dr. Saf has successfully liberated numberless individuals from tribulation so that they continue to lead a fruitful and inspiring life. His process, The Buxy Recovery Process, will liberate thousands of people from their burdens.

He is a recovered addict, an abuse victim, and above all a survivor. Saf can candidly talk about his experiences to help others liberate themselves from the attachments to any addiction- food, drugs, sex, technology and more. His approach incorporated modalities that identify the subconscious reasons for the undesired behavior, which reveals the path to healing and brings hope for a better future.

His shows include Saf Talks, MensTalk -a Feel Good Factor TV show on SKY Showcase 191, and a show on Spirituality Gone Wild. He also co-founded a Non-Profit, which has earned him the following awards:

Global Humanitarian Award
Global Change Maker (LOANI & World Leaders Association)
MENTORx
Dr Sarvepalli Radhakrishnan Award (Award of Honor)
The Black Blazer Award

THE GOLD RIBBON AWARD OF LEADERSHIP, EXCELLENCE AND ACHIEVEMENT
Breakthrough International Bible University
An honorary Doctorate Degree in Humane Letters

Saf's new book, Out of the Madness: A Message of Hope was published in March 2021. This autobiography is written to help others wake up out of their unhealthy habits to see their gifts.

Dr. Saf Buxy
www.safbuxy.com

CHAPTER 5

Endings and Beginnings

Dr. Sofie Nubani

The most profound moment of my life is when I had a true soul wake-up call. It was one that felt very hurtful and very disappointing at that time. It almost made me feel like my past life was like being part of a movie scene until that moment, only to see all the characters changing roles. This was from close family members to friends. I felt like it was another world, one that I was not familiar with and was very cold.

After my mom passed away a lot of changes in my family dynamics also changed.Never underestimate a strong mother, women, and wife role in a household. For the first time ever I truly felt alone, this time it was after the end of my just over two years marriage.

Was the world just changing to a very unfamiliar way or was it just my new reality? I come from a very family-oriented culture and background but what I was experiencing was a lot of separation and distance, not in miles or locations, but in hearts and communications.

It was not long before I realized I was living in my new reality.

I must say it was hard to observe. The closest description of how I felt was experiencing the emotion of abandonment and wow!!! I just truly realized the true feeling I was living at that time, this moment as I am writing.

As children, we grow to believe what our parents, teachers, respected elders taught us, we then grow and from their teachings, the environment surrounding us and our personal experiences we form our own confirmation biases. We start choosing and making decisions influenced by our cognitive association formation.

Well to me after so many years of respecting and honoring my cultural background and family traditions, I for the first time started questioning my beliefs about them.

What I was raised to believe about a family unit, togetherness, and support was becoming completely confusing, contradicting, and conditional.

When I was going through my personal experience of dark moments in my life, I felt alone and shocked by the behavior of the people closest to me.

I could not understand their attitude or all the guiding principles they once had embedded in me. I had made decisions, cut off relationships, even lived in places because I loved them and wanted to be close to them, please them and be accepted by them.

These people were my family. Where and how could they just disappear like that? My soul felt heavy and unclear. I was going through a divorce at that time and the person that usually listened, advised and was there for me the most was in heaven. My mom. Ijust did not realize the difference her presence made in my life till I experienced her absence.

Where are my other family members? Friends? Anyone!

I was an emotional basket and never felt more alone. My heart was heavy, sad, and blocked.

A little history about my personality

You see, growing up I was extremely curious and equally sensitive.

You would think by being so sensitive, I would have a shy personality, one that is less curious and quieter, but I did not.

One day, I remember my teacher yelling at me, I was in high school. She was telling me to stop talking, a few of us were talking at that moment but my name was the only one called out loud. I remember my tears silently rolling over my face instantly. I was quiet for the rest of the year in her class.

It was not only if someone yelled at me that my soul felt disturbed but also if I was listening to someone yelling at another in my presence. I did not like conflicts even if I was witnessing them by others.

Fast forward

Working on myself for years, I practiced thought awareness that led me to become better at regulating and managing my emotions. I then started becoming more self aware, my resilience, tolerance and willpower levels increased. It was not easy to upset me anymore like it was in the past.

Reading books like The Four Agreements by Don Miguel Ruiz, who reveals the source of self-limiting beliefs that rob us of joy and guide us to unlearn the beliefs, expectations, and agreements that lead to needless suffering improved my life perspective and helped me to understand myself and others better?

Agreement 1:

Be Impeccable with Your Word.

Agreement 2: Don't Take Anything Personally.

Agreement 3: Don't Make Assumptions.

Agreement 4: Always Do Your Best.

Later I learned about

Agreement 5: BE SKEPTICAL, BUT LEARN TO LISTEN

I loved the four agreements and later the faith agreement, I started applying them more in my life.

I started becoming more intentional and conscious in the way I let my day, the results were noticed, I was transitioning, transforming, and transcending.

I developed emotional toughness. That came with lots of practice and positive self-discipline. I had to feel deep pain with all my senses, then I had to try to understand it, accept it and respect the lessons it came to teach. That was not easy at that time.

Reflecting today at those dark moments I understand much better their purpose. The meaning became clearer. It helped me tap into my spiritual intelligence and develop my emotional toughness.

What helped me the most during that period was my faith, self-love, self-respect, self-honor, and my refusal to ABANDON me.

I learned how to be there for myself and by that, I mean, how I was to myself, a best cheerleader, friend, encourager, and comforter.

I realized that in life there is one constant and that is, "change" therefore we must be flexible and adaptable enough as it arrives especially when this change is not what we had planned or wished for.

When I got married for the second time after many years of being single my goal and intention was not to be divorced but I did and that also taught me a valuable lesson and that was; I had to stay focused on my direction and not original goal,

Such awareness helped me to adapt, and course correct my thoughts as well my attitude.

I was more clear and mentally focused. I was allowing new beginnings to unfold with more ease and peace as I was facing such a big life event.

Simply focusing on my direction and not the goal helped me transition better and faster when things moved to different directions and went contrary to my plans.

Time truly allowed me to understand many new emotions that were visiting after my divorce.

These emotions were not pleasant, but they became my best teacher. It is much easier writing about them today than living them by the minute.

Let me tell you going through disappointments as a child while I still had my family, a roof over my head, siblings to talk to and interact with, parents that provided all our basic needs and more is a lot easier than going through shocks, disappointments and heartaches as an adult when since then your whole life and family dynamic has changed, especially if you had become very independent and more introverted.

I had my moments of insecurities, doubts, and uncertainties. They all surrounded me during that period I felt I was in an emotional bondage and suffering. I was not free.

(While studying for my Neurolinguistic Programming (NLP) certification program. I learned a lot about myself and understood better my emotions and what I had experienced in my life that back then was not clear. I learned through an exercise we did in class that FREEDOM was an emotional core value to me. It was such a helpful exercise. I had a breakthrough moment that forever changed the way I look at things as well as understand myself. I do recommend NLP for anyone reading this, especially if you are interested to know your emotional core values, your pain values, and your gain values as they will help you go through life with more clarity and understanding)

For me, I realized that without freedom, I could not feel peace.

To get clearer I asked myself some questions...

Do I want to be a victim of my circumstance or a victor over them?

Do I want to spend the rest of my life feeling sorry for things I have no control of or do I want to create a healthier environment for myself?

Do I want to be a slave to my mind, or do I want it to be my servant?

Taking a shortcut was not the solution

At that time, to live the life I was accustomed to and avoid all the challenges of my new life changes that I had to deal with, I had to just obey my family's conditional request which was to go back and live in Jordan and have my dad's full support A to Z.

You see, I come from a culture where a man always is the provider to his wife, daughter or sister when/if needed. That would have been the easiest thing to do if I wanted to take a shortcut to end the struggle I was going through.

The request was conditional and made my heart feel even more blocked.

Taking such action would make me feel helpless, hopeless, and upset. Knowing that I was not able to pick myself up or live in a country that accommodated my ambition and my soul felt most liberated would make me feel like I abandoned myself.

Growing up I always loved the United States of America and every time I visited with my family, usually for the summer holidays, I would feel sad when we had to leave.

Going back conflicted with my emotional core value of freedom, which I learned was very important for my overall well-being.

Freedom was something that I valued and could never compromise.

My conclusion

When you honor your truth, speak your truth, and live your truth you will feel free and live with inner peace.

As I reflected on my life going through all these changes, I realized that all past choices I made including ones that caused me to suffer were made in honor of my soul's freedom.

In the beginning I could fairly say it was challenging, however, it sure paid off in the long term!

At least I can say, I wrote the manuscript of the story of my life with my own pen, and words.

I loved my family but couldn't live my life conforming to passed down traditions and culture rules that were applied from thousands of years ago and based on technology and lifestyle that then exited.

Today I am a global citizen, I still honor my culture as well many others; however, I have learned through my own experience and spiritual journey truths that have directed me to the wisdom of my own soul.

My higher consciousness and inner compass have made me more mindful and aware of how I live my life and what is more important to me according to my own journey based on my personal life experiences.

I learned that all the sleepless nights were a cosmic alarm clock awakening my soul to a discovery of one of the most important laws of the universe: the law of detachment.

I learned that a lot of my answers were all explained just from reflecting on the process of birth and death.

I learned about my connection to the word freedom. I mean when I just hear that word, my whole soul lightens up. I breathe better and feel lighter.

My clear understanding of the word freedom arose one day as I was driving to the beach feeling a little heavy. I took my notepad and a pen.I learned a lot about myself that day.

I remember asking myself what does the word freedom mean to me, why am I so connected to it, and how can I always live feeling free?

What came to me was:

When we are born the umbilical cord is cut immediately after birth. A mother is a supporter, yet we were not meant to remain attached. When we die, we die alone and that no one, not even our parents, spouse, children, or siblings accompanies us in our graves.

That by the law of nature, creation, and the universe we are meant to be free as we are born, and it is how we leave. I learned that there is much wisdom to be extracted from that. Then I asked, how could one achieve the true meaning of freedom?

What came to me are the "CHOICES" we make in our life that led us to where we end up. Then I asked how I could make choices that would make me feel free. The answer that I received was that 1st, I had to be "CONVINCED" on "WHY" I was making these choices and then 2nd, convinced in the choices made. Then I asked, if I believe in my choices and am convinced about them then why did I have to suffer when I did. The answer that came to me then was "COURAGE"! You must have courage to act.

To live in my body I needed peace, and to create that peace, I had to have courage and to build my courage I simply had to make choices that made me feel freer.

WOW! I not only knew I had this special connection to the word "freedom" but I now understood how to achieve it in my life as it was divinely guided and broken down to me in moments of stillness, contemplation and reflection.

I highly recommend making time to connect and center away from all the background noise and distractions of your life. I remember driving back from the beach that day feeling so light as if someone carried me all the way back home.

I learned with my experience how to transform the feeling of loneliness to creative adventure and the feelings of fear or anger into curiosity.

I understood later why I was meant to be so alone and disconnected from everything including people that I was so closely connected with. It was in this period of my life when I discovered my true powers.

What helped me overcome my heart block I went to seminars, workshops, and when I couldn't afford to go, I would listen to YouTube videos of mentors that inspired me. That helped expand my mind and helped me see things from a different perspective).

I learned how to optimize my creative mindset and to stay on a higher level of thinking.

I tapped into my creativity and applied different thinking styles when I had to solve

problems and find solutions.

I learned about strategic communication and applied the teaching.

-Identify my goals

-Understand my audience

-Share my values

-Express my needs

I developed a strong self-concept

In areas of my:

Self-Image

Self Confidence

& My Ideal Self the self I aspire to be

I used Vision, Action and Dream Boards to stay on track with my goals and desired outcomes.

I learned more in-depth about the law of detachment, one that helped me to truly evolve and practice unconditional love. I learned the importance of being open to everything and attached to nothing.

I have a grown, handsome, and smart independent son who I am so proud of and blessed to have, Rawy Rayan who I pray for success, peace, wisdom, and good health over his life. He is a young man who is focused with great leadership skills, he now is not my young child anymore. He has his life and purpose to fulfill.

Having a child is a beautiful gift, yet I learned our children are not our own as they are also meant to be free.

I also used my intellectual curiosity as my best friend, in times of fear or anger I would become more interested in finding out why

I'm feeling a certain way or someone else is feeling a certain way if they are the reason for my anger or fear. I had more empathy as well practiced self-compassion.

I would ask myself more questions like what, when, why, how to get clearer or find more about something or someone.

I prayed, meditated, and journaled; I was able to forgive the people that hurt me the most.

I asked myself often prior to making any decision:

Does this make me feel free?

I knew when I felt free I had inner peace, based on my answer I then took action.

I played more with my two angle cats Giovanni and Valentino

In this period. I evolved so much and faster than I ever can recall.

You see all the times I invested in myself paid off in good dividends.

Self-Lead

You see, if you want to maintain a beautiful outdoors to your home, you will need to pay attention to your landscaping, possibly your pool and so forth. To keep your grass nice and trim you will need the right tools to keep it up. If you want your pool to look good and stay clean you need the right tools to do that. Without the proper equipment and materials that won't be possible.

Just like if someone has a heart attack and needs an immediate open-heart surgery, just knowing the right doctor or going to the best hospital is not going to be enough.

They also need the right tools for the surgeon to work with.

It's the same thing in life; you need the right tools to use, depending on the issues you're facing or circumstances you're dealing with.

Be prepared as well alert. Have your tools ready. You are your best investment. The best gift you can share with your loved ones and humanity, is living the best version of yourself.

Being single has allowed me to get busy with projects I enjoyed and the freedom I needed to truly be clear on my purpose. It allowed me to connect with my heavenly gifts, to be able to see them and open them.

I love uplifting, encouraging, empowering, and relaxing people as well as making them laugh.

I love to remind people to walk into their own magnificence, to claim their own power and not to let anything or anyone rob their inner peace. I love to remind people to let their smile change the world, not the world changes their smile.

Being in service is a passion to my heart. It is what allowed me to heal, grow and evolve.

I was able to build such a great relationship with myself. Emotional Mastery is an everyday practice for me.

I learned that happiness was not a destination but a daily practice, and could be accomplished by simply choosing one positive, more empowering thought over a negative disempowering one and that is not supportive to my self-transcendence journey.

I had outgrown some relationships and eliminated some toxic ones. I learned to be true to what supports my highest good and to be more selective in whom I allow in my inner circle.

I learned that being in service is my soul calling as I always heard that inner voice saying: I am a servant of light (that I shall honor). However, whom I surround myself with daily are those who I feel have authentic integrity and possess qualities that resonate and are aligned with my soul's core; those with a growth mindset, genuine influence, think critically, are humble and seeking to do better, they have empathy and are good in self leading, these people don't grow older, they grow up with time.

When they say: "You are who you surround yourself with" there is much truth to it. Be very mindful of who you receive, share and exchange energy from, to and with.

Raise your standards and do not settle for anything less than what you are deserving of. You can never replace time that you lost or buy inner peace. It is your everyday choices only that can support you to maximize and optimize living the best version of you. Choose wisely!

My personal challenges including cultural differences and religious beliefs, helped me expand my vision and perceptions, understand things beyond just the physical. I meditated often and that helped me to have an expanded conscious perception. I valued the principles of interfaith harmony and cross-cultural harmony.

The more connected I was with myself the more aware and clear I felt. "Know thyself" a quote by Socrates that is of great wisdom to follow.

I had spent many days alone and learned more and more about my life and myself. I had experienced the joy of soul searching and going to deeper and higher realms.

It was clear to me that we experience sadness, depression, stress and more, when we stop laughing, growing, learning, creating, and living our best potential.

I like to end by some quotes by Maya Angelou that often inspired me when facing any life challenges.

"If you don't like something, change it. If you can't change it, change your attitude."

"It's one of the greatest gifts you can give yourself, to forgive. Forgive everybody."

"We may encounter many defeats, but we must not be defeated."

Blessings and Namaste
Dr. Sofie Nubani
Creatrix Interpersonal Executive Coach

DR. SOFIE NUBANI

Dr. Sofie Nubani is a Interpersonal-Executive Coach| Public Speaker| International Creative Mindset Strategist| NLP Trainer| Honorary Doctor of Divinity| Honorary Doctorate in Philosophy in Metaphysics| 3xBest-Selling Author| Founder of the Circle of Creative Masters Institute & The Athena Coaching (Spiritual Development) program| Global Advisor and Educator| Co-Host Online Live Show "Wisdom Café"| Program Chair of MEETx a speaking platform inspired by TEDx| Executive President of Charles Walters Society for Innovation and Research.

Her recently released book "Optimize Your Creative Mindset" is an award winner and Best-Seller. Along with Dr. Bob Choat, she is the Co-Founder of the "Laughter Mindset Experience" & "M.E.T.A. Shift Program."

As a Creative Mindset Strategist, she approaches new box thinking and answers along with higher thinking styles when offering creative solutions on hot topics being addressed.

CERTIFICATIONS:

* Certified NLP Trainer
*Certified Life Coach
*Certified Reiki Master
*Certified Motivational Speaker
* Certified EFT/TFT Practitioner
*Certified Laughter Yoga Instructor
*Speaking Facilitator Transformational Services
*Certified Social & Emotional Intelligence Coach

Her unique coaching style assists people to release emotional pain,and reach a higher mental state.

PUBLICATIONS:

Optimize Your Creative Mindset: Award Winner & Best-Seller
Quarentena and Beyond by Ada Gartenmann
The Global Achievers,,One Tribe, From My Mama's Kitchen and
Thrive Global Magazine

EDUCATION:

Doctorate in Spiritual Development (DSD)
Diploma in Innovation Management

AWARDS:

* Humanitarian Awards (3) * Goodwill ambassador
* Advocate of Interfaith Harmony * MENTORx from Government of India

* Blue blazer of Global Excellence Performance
* Stellar Achievements from All Woman Rock by CD Wilson Events
* Outstanding Creative Mindset Strategies and Youth Development Skills by IYBC
* International Corona Warrior Award by Anti-Corruption Foundation of India
* Best Achievement Award 2021for promoting United Nations Sustainable Goals in the Community by Dr. Naveed Anju founder of EWV
* Gold Medal Educator award and Best International World Speaker by Doza Serkja Macedonian association.
* Youth Icon award in the category of Entrepreneur and Author by Trinetra Film Production's
* International Coordinator and Corona Warriors Award 2021 by All India Real for Cultural Educational Welfare Society
* Title Holder of World Book of Records, London 2021

To learn more about Dr. Sofie Nubani, visit
https://www.circleofcreativemasters.com/
Email :nubanisofie@gmail.com
Website: drsofienubani.com

CHAPTER 6

Dominate the Decade and become the Change Maker; GET TO WORK. GET IT DONE!

Ragne Sinikas

Don't postpone your greatness! Overcome your heart blocks and become the Change Maker that influences, impacts, inspires and invests in yourself and in others. Reach your mountain top of victory and live your gifts and talents. Do the work that fuels your soul.

As you read those lines I am sure that you are fully awake and present in your own life. I assume the reason you have this book in hand is that you know there is unleashed potential within you and you want more out of your life. You want to grow as a person. Maybe you are looking to grow as a leader who produces epic results that take your company to the next level. Maybe, you have this book in hand because you feel stuck, procrastination holds you back, or you have a strong desire to become the "CHANGE MAKER" of your life and business.

On January 20th 1999, I was 17 years old , I realized that my boyfriend was gone forever. He died and it wasn't a dream. I was left alone with no income, knowledge, or tools for survival and a lot of bills. After 4 tranquilizer induced days, I realized that I could be a victim of the circumstance or I could make the decision to take responsibility for my life right then.

At that moment, I said to myself, "This is my life. Right here, right now! I have a choice. Ragne, you can either continue with what is not working and repeat it until you die or you can make the decision to actually change your life. There is no in-between."

You see, when this moment comes in your life take the responsibility for your experience of being alive. If you are unhappy, struggling and plain miserable, own it. Step up the ownership of where you are and where you are headed. Look at where you suck the most and declare a change. Get to work, get it done. Too overwhelming? Get to work, get it done. Do something, do anything, even in small steps. Changes happen when you begin to change what you do.

"The greatest lie in life is telling yourself you don't belong and that you are not enough. Wake up, because if you want to be great, don't do your best, do whatever it takes." - JT Foxx.

After a while, I began to understand that the only thing that was "stuck" about me was my self-talk. I realized that I became my conversations. I couldn't see the woods from the trees. My fear and self doubt was dominating my life until I realized that I have self doubts, but I don't have to be defined by them. I have a past, but I do not have to be defined by it. It is a senseless waste of a life to carve the remarkable marvel of what it is to be alive down to bad habits and complaints. It would be a shame to realize the number of mediocre years, weeks, and days wasted focused on the wrong thing when these could have been purposeful and full of inspiration. You are a sphere for life to happen, a fierce and astonishing environment for wonder and adversity and everything in between. You are a rare moment, a unique blast in a burst of time that echoes and then disappears into the chasm. You are a marvel of being and it's time for you to start acting like one. Get to work, get it done.

We live in a new generation of wealth and success. There are so many addictions out there that affect us consciously or unconsciously.

When I started to pay attention to this, things started to change. I realized that I was addicted to certainty. I needed to understand that certainty does not exist - it's a myth handed down from generation to generation. I have learned to embrace this world of uncertainty and fight for the life I really want. I have asked myself so many times why in the moments when we are the closest to falling apart we are able to actually fall together? Do we really need to have a dramatic event in our life in order to have the courage and strength to live the life we want and deserve? No we don't. Awaken yourself now! This is your time. I can't save you, you need to understand that only you have the power to save yourself from a mediocre life that does not satisfy you. Our lives become blurred and confused by the constant pressure of expectations. The worst expectations are the ones we put into the mix ourselves. Real freedom and power appear when you free yourself from them.

Have you noticed we live in a world that has an addiction to distraction? So many people are chasing those shiny things. I really get it, I have felt the same thing. In order to belong or have a status, you get the feeling that you need to have it all as well. Fortunately I was awakened. The best discovery is to understand that an addiction is the death of your creative production. You need to protect your focus every single day as the industry makes you addicted to it. Our devices excel at keeping us from seeing the world around us. Instead of navigating daily tasks such as having your full attention at the breakfast table with your loved ones or enjoying nature or laser focusing on your business, we have our eyes fixed on our phone. I am guilty of being a slave to my phone and giving it more attention than anything else. It was really affecting my family. I made a decision there, at that moment, when my son asked me something and I answered, honey give me 5 minutes. He answered I don't need you in 5 minutes, I need you now. I froze, stopped everything and took the responsibility of being present in that very moment. I promised myself to act according to my values and priorities to focus on things that matter the most. I was in shock and ashamed of myself, he was only 7 years old and he was the one that gave me a very valuable lesson on my values, priorities and how those were reflected in real life. Since that day I am not just trying to put my phone away but I really do. I actually take time to look around. The most important thing that I want you to understand is to be present in every moment that has been given to you. Don't take those moments for granted.

What does it take to see what no one else sees? I describe this skill as creativity, and we live in a world that celebrates it. But finding a solution to a particularly tricky problem or discovering a world changing idea that produces an epic profit, like Change Makers do, takes more than creativity. So stop talking and get it done. The secret of success is determined by our daily agenda. It all comes down to what we do today. You see, success doesn't just suddenly occur one day. Every day of our life is merely preparation for the next. What you become is the result of what you do today. Growth, success, and fulfillment come from making wise decisions on the priorities for our life and then managing them well in our daily agenda. You begin to build a better life by being determined to make good decisions, but that alone is not enough. You need to know what priorities to set for your life. Start with the morning routine. The titans of business fully understand that the way you begin your day sets up the caliber of your focus and the quality of your performance. To dominate your domain you absolutely need to learn the daily rituals of epic performers. Once you do, nothing will ever be the same for you.

We are always seeking for the life work balance but do we really measure what it means and what it takes to have it? Let me give you my definition and what really works for me. My interior powerhouse is a balance of my mind, soul, heart and health. I call it the most important part of the Golden Ratio of Life Circle. Those four elements are also what the "Change Makers" need to have in perfect equilibrium to unleash their full potential and operate in their peak performance. In this chapter we will focus on one thing, the mind. So every morning at 5:00 AM, if you take that miracle hour and spend 60 minutes working on your mind, heart, health and soul, you consistently improve yourself. You become more focused, productive, brave, and of so much service to the world that you cannot help but change it.

When it comes to the key focus areas of the mind I put my attention to the following: reading and learning, conversations, influences, environments, performances, reflections, visualization, meditation.

Read every morning for at least 60 minutes or listen to the audios of the mentors and role models. It will set your day and your life! Be curious, ask questions and learn something new daily.

Did you know that we become our conversations? Your sense of personal power is directly related to the strength of the relationship between you and what you say. We ignore our promises as a source of personal power. Turning your life around will require you to start keeping your promises. The promises that you have been given to yourself are meaningless and the reason is down to a lifetime of bending, breaking, changing, and abandoning your promises. Over time, the relationship to what you say has become vague, it lacks any real substance or personal power. This is why your life is not working! When I look back into my life I have to admit that every personal failure was a result of a broken promise. It's all you and your promises, everything else is noise. You need to focus on yourself and be congruent. The way we think is very important. Most people give too much significance to what's going on in their heads. I remember so vividly the dialog that I had with myself on the day that determined my destiny. Ragne, who are you and what is your life purpose? Are you going to be defined by the circumstances? I had all the good reasons and excuses to just give up, move back to the small town with my parents and give up my dream to become an attorney. I decided to have no doubts, fear or excuses, I chose to fight for my dream. Be the person that does not follow the trajectory of self-doubt, fear, considerations, and plain old fashion superstition. Unfortunately the majority of people are struggling with excuses and self-doubts. Life only changes the paradigm of action. That's it. If you want to change, do differently than you did before. You are not your thoughts, get to work and get it done! Act now! If you do not believe in yourself, then why should anyone else believe in you? I have learned through my personal story that the way I see myself determines the way I behave. Knowing that, I started to notice that we always act in alignment of how we see ourselves. Now I understand that my daily behavior always reflects my deepest beliefs. Our environment has a bigger impact and influence on our life than I would like to admit.To Have the results that only 5% of the population have, you've got to be thinking, then behaving, then living like only 5% of the population are willing to think, behave and live. Get comfortable being uncomfortable. What does it take from you to constantly operate outside your comfort zone? You're never going to rise any higher than you think. So how do we become that rare 5%? Based on my experience I had to change my thinking, I had to do the work, I did whatever it took, and I never quit on myself. I had to change my environment and that had a huge impact. I was doing the same things, the same way with the same people and surprise surprise the results were the same. Until I learned that I had to surround myself with people that wanted me to succeed and they were more experienced than me, they belonged to this 5% of the population. We become our conversations and we behave like the people around us. The best advice I can give you is to learn from your coach, from role models and from the icons and titans of history. Your thinking and performance, even your financial and physical life is influenced by your friends and by their friends. All the toxic people and the energy vampires you have in your life are destroying your fortunes. So if you want to be an epic performer look for a mentor that has proven results. If you want to earn a million, look for someone that has done it. Don't ask advice from your relatives who have no experience in those fields. The key to success is to find the right coach or mentor to double your income and your impact, triple your investment in your personal growth and in your professional capabilities. Residual wisdom comes from coaching. The marketplace always pays for what's best.

We have to have our place and time for reflections. Reflection allows you to know yourself. The epic "Change Makers' 'spends time in the world but they also make time for the wilderness. There is a huge value of reflection, a huge value of daily contemplation. Your faith has to be larger than your fear. Fear is the main reason that holds you back and causes inaction. Nobody will believe in you until you believe in yourself. Leadership begins within you. Your outer life reflects your interior identity. Persistency is when you have mastered your interior life and by doing it you become invincible. Everything is going to come from what' s going on within you. Your relationships reflect your self-relationship. Everything begins within!

"Limitation is nothing more than a mentality that too many good people practice daily until they believe it's reality. It breaks my heart to see so many potentially powerful human beings stuck in a story about why they can't be extraordinary, professionally and personally. You need to remember that your excuses are seducers, your fears are liars and your doubts are thieves."

- Robin Sharma.

Visualize what you want. Picture everything you want so clearly in your mind, until you can see it right in front of you. Write it all down on a piece of paper and create a vision board, then you will have evidence in the future. Evidence of the amazing power of your mind, the amazing power of you. If all you ever do is live by what is in front of you, reacting to the life in front of you, you will never move beyond the life that is in front of you. You have to be able to see outside of your current situation. You must be able to acknowledge where you are in life. But now, you are capable of creating so much more. Know that where you are right now is not your life. You are where you are right now because of your past decisions and your past beliefs. Now it is the time to sum up the courage to ask for better, to believe in better, to believe magic is on the way. Now it's time to get what you deserve. In life we don't get what we ask for. We get what we ask and work for. Nothing in life will work without work. No books. No seminars. No audio tapes. No gurus. Nothing. Nothing will work if you don't. Get to work, get it done!

What you want is not going to come to you by just dreaming about it. When you get in your car to go somewhere, you would never expect to arrive at the destination by just closing your eyes and dreaming about it. You know you can not get there instantly. You must know where you're going but you also understand that right now you are here, and in order to get to your destination there is going to be a journey. There might be roadblocks, detours, stop signs, even breakdowns. But if you really must get to that destination, you can and will find a way. You would never stop half way and turn around because of a detour, a setback or an obstacle. You just take whatever path leads to your destination, even if it wasn't the path you planned on taking. Even if it was not the easiest path. Life is no different. If you want something...anything in your life you must first know where you are and then you must know what it is going to take to get there. Get to work, get it done!

You need to make a commitment that no matter what happens I will reach that destination. If I have to go the long way I will go the long way. If I have to learn a new way, I will learn a new way. If there are detours, roadblocks or break downs. I will keep going, I will fix the issue, get patched up, and I will never quit. If you just know, if you just believe, you will get there and you have the courage to see it through. There is nothing you can not have, nowhere you can't go and no one you can not become.

Muhammed Ali said: "The man who has no imagination has no wings."

If you can not envision it, if you can not believe it, you will never see it, you will never be it. You see, if you want to live an average life that is fine, keep your feet on the ground, but if you want to soar, if you want to achieve great things, you must not only think those crazy thoughts but feel it. Feel what it would feel like to be doing that thing you want to do.Feel what it feels like to have all the things you want. To be the person that has achieved the things you want to achieve. The very process of you feeling like you already have it will send vibrational signals to your brain and if you are willing to work for it, it will be in your life very soon. Get to work, get it done!

Albert Einstein once said: "Imagination is everything. It is the preview of life's coming attractions."

Only those who believe that anything is possible can achieve the things most would consider impossible. You must know who you are going to be, before you become that person. You must picture what you want to achieve and feel like you already have it, before you can bring it into your reality.

In the greatest book of all time, Think and grow Rich, Napoleon Hill states:

"Whatever the mind of man can conceive and believe, it can achieve. You are the master of your destiny. You can influence, direct and control your own environment. You can make your life what you want it to be."

It's not a magic trick. It's not a new philosophy. Most of you know about it and if you do not, you should start paying attention, because just about anyone who is great knows about it.

As Robin Sharma said: "Everything is created twice, first in the mind and then in reality."

There is an energy and power far greater than we can comprehend at play and we can either use it, live in harmony with it, create with it or run in fear from it.

Not long ago I was asked what my life purpose was and what is the legacy that I want to leave behind. Today I have a burning desire to add value, passion for helping others and clarity of vision. I am devoted to my mission, to empower through education and I make my imaginings a reality. I invite you to overcome your heart blocks today and start living the life you deserve.

RAGNE SINIKAS

Mrs Ragne Sinikas is a seasoned entrepreneur. She is the Founder of the World Women Conference & Awards (WWCA), SendHerDeals.com, Complex Holding, Starpreneurs TV, Untold Story Foundation, Change Makers Coach, Public Speaker, Philanthropist.

Ragne's acute awareness throughout the years has provided her with the ability to contribute with her heart and soul to helping everyone she meets. Ragne insight of working in many countries has built bridges of communication strengthening initiatives between women and local and state government.

Ragne was born into a country under the control of the Soviet Union, where there was no civil rights. The impact of her childhood has set a solid foundation on her quest for women empowerment in education, health and civil rights.

Ragne courage is always present in every step of her life, always building teams of loyal woman that champion and help the less fortunate girls and women. Ragne strength and inspiration is powered by the energy and accomplished of every women she helps.

Ragne firm commitment of achieving empowerment through education is key to Obtaining gender equality. Ragne involvement with university students in Mexico has inspired many to participate in multiplying the gender equality movement.

Ragne works with kids who have health challenges such as the need for heart surgeries. With over 100 surgeries in last 24 months, she has changed the life of 100 families. 100 women that had lost hope and now have a healthy kid with a strong heart and an amazing future.

Ragne passion is helping Women. Ragne Energy is the beat of her heart and soul in every action she sets forth. Today, Ragne builds global partnerships with the vision of establishing local chapters in Estonia, USA and Mexico that promote and accomplish gender equality and empowerment.

Ragne's passion is serving others and making significant impact to the lives that she touches. Therefore Ragne is the advisory board member for the Ellamo Foundation and an active member of several Non Profit Asociations and Foundations; The Asociacion de Mujeres Empresarias and FCEM, Red Autismo Foundation and Corazon de Niño Foundation, Cadena A.C. Foundation is a nonprofit organisation dedicated to assist in emergencies and prevention of natural disasters. Coparmex Delegacion Los Cabos, Rochat School Los Cabos, The Worldwide Association of Female Professionals, ambassador for The Global Access Initiative (GAI).

https://allmylinks.com/ragne-sinikas

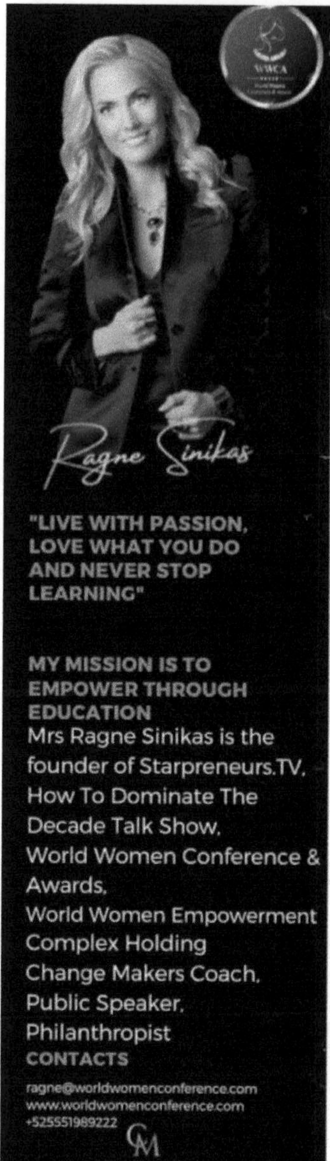

Ragne Sinikas

is a social entrepreneur, Founder of the World Women Empowerment (WWE), World Women Conference & Awards (WWCA), Starpreneurs.TV, Complex Holding. Philanthropist, International speaker, coach & co-author, global award winner

WHO IS RAGNE? :

Mrs. Ragne Sinikas is a social entrepreneur, philanthropist, an advanced online marketer focused on helping brands go from presence to profit. Founder of World Women Empowerment, Starpreneurs.tv, Real Estate Developer, an International speaker, coach of the Change Makers and co-author of various international best sellers, global award winner with her Dominate the Decade Podcast and the winner of the Women in Business Network by Wintrade Global.

Ragne is the founder of the World Women Empowerment that is an international initiative of the Untold Story Foundation dedicated to humanitarian assistance and community development. The WWE is focused on women empowerment through education, skills building and entrepreneurial programs that create new opportunities for women to sustain their livelihoods. Ragne is social entrepreneur who pursues novel applications that have the potential to solve community-based problems. Ragne is a partner in companies that are engaged in social justice, environmental sustainability, and alternative energy/clean technology efforts like Avantu Global, Renwol and Cannativo Indigenous hands movement.

Ragne is an international public speaker, co-author of various international best sellers for entrepreneurs. Ragne is a seasoned entrepreneur with 15 years of sales leadership in developing and implementing sales and business plans throughout Mexico, Finland, the Baltics, Russia, Italy, and Germany in several industry sectors. Originally from Estonia and now residing in Los Cabos, Mexico, Ragne is a multilingual world citizen. She earned a bachelor's degree in Business Administration, specializing in marketing at the International University of Audentes, Estonia. Ragne's passion is serving others and making significant impact to the lives that she touches. Therefore Ragne is the advisory board member for the Ellamo Foundation and an active member of several Non Profit Asociations and Foundations: The Asociacion de Mujeres Empresarias and FCEM, Red Autismo Foundation and Corazon de Niño Foundation, Cadena A.C. Foundation, Coparmex Delegacion Los Cabos, Rochat School Los Cabos, The Worldwide Association of Female Professionals, The Ambassador for Mexico at World Leader Summit, Member of Ancestral Nations A.c. Cannativo movement of indigenous hands, development for a sustainable ecosystem within the indigenous communities of Mexico hand in hand with the native tribes of Baja California Sur.

CHAPTER 7

Words that Bind

Michelle Mras

"Sticks and stones may break my bones,
but words will never hurt me."
– Anonymous

annoying
ridiculous
idiot
stupid
fat
short
slow
gangly
awkward
tramp

scrawny
ugly
useless
lazy
no good
not good enough
waste of time
hate you
no one wants you
Wish you were never BORN!

Degrading comments. Sometime throughout your life you've seen, heard or uttered these words. Were they directed at you? Did you direct them to someone else?

Did you say them to yourself? Do you still?

I blocked my heart from receiving love and acceptance from not one incident, but from a collection of perceptions over a lifetime.

In my youth, the statement about words never hurting made sense. Now, that I am older and wiser, I have learned from life experiences that physical pain eventually fades. The hurtful words do not. It is difficult to detach our psyche from pondering and building upon them like foundational bricks in our personal prisons of self-doubt. They erode our confidence and how we relate to other people in our lives. No one can devalue who you are without your permission.

Words are powerful. Be careful how you use them and how you perceive them.

Throughout my youth, I heard simple words from various individuals. Inadvertently, I gathered statements and words directed at me or to others around me to define who I believed I was. I took each statement and word to create a mountain of bricks in which I built my fortress of safety. Why would anyone choose to place themselves in a prison of negativity? Perhaps it was a comfort zone for myself where I could live my life from a point of lack. I can't fail if I am not worthy of anything.

How about you? Have you built an invisible wall around you? Have you taken the time to examine the sources? As a coach, professional speaker and author, I have dedicated many years of my life pondering the origins of my comfort zone. In particular, I had twenty-four (plus) months of self-study when I obtained a traumatic brain injury and was trapped in my brain unable to communicate or walk without assistance. I had nothing better to do, but to self-examine my life. What I discovered was that my bricks of self-doubt were not built out of concrete, but rather sand.

One of my early memories is of my grandfather entering our home. I was about 5-years old. Grandpa would enter the front door and begin a long list of accolades and praising of how much he loved me. He would continue the list until he found me. So it became our game. I would hide from him so he would have to come up with more words. We had a wonderful game that only the two of us played. When he finally found me, usually because I was giggling uncontrollably, he would whisk me up into the air, twirl me around, bring me close into a big bear hug as he proceeded to shower me with kisses which ended with tickles. We would always end up on the ground giggling and telling each other how much we missed each other. I still get teary eyed thinking of the immense amount of love my grandfather showered upon me.

One day, one of my cousins was visiting our home when Grandpa came into our house and we began our game. My cousin told me that Grandpa only did that because he felt sorry for me, because no one really loved me. As Grandpa came searching for me while calling out accolades, I felt deflated. When he found me, I was in tears because I believed he only pretended to love me. Grandpa assured me that he surely loved me, but my young mind allowed the one negative thought spoken by a jealous cousin to ruin my bliss. Thousands of praises were eliminated with one negative thought; just like the saying, "one bad apple spoils the others". From that day onward, I played the game with grandpa, but in the back of my mind, I doubted his sincerity.

A few short years later, he passed away. I distinctly remember thinking that he left me alone. He promised to always be with me and he left without taking me. I concluded that people who love me will leave me.

My childhood was spent as a military "brat" that lived overseas in my mother's country of birth, the Philippines. I am the fourth child of six children. I have three older siblings, a six-year gap to me, then a 10-year gap to the twins. Our family got along well. We kids spent quality time together and generally enjoyed each other. That said, we were always being compared. Not as a negative, rather, it's how we were identified.

The eldest brother was praised for being a talented musician. The next eldest brother was praised for his athletic abilities. The third, my elder sister, was praised for her natural grace and beauty. Then, there was me. I was okay at what the other three were great at, but not stellar. The youngest twins were too little to be part of the equation at the time. My siblings were being introduced to a house guest with each of their attributes being highlighted. When my father got to me, he said, "... and this is Michelle. She's smart". No animated descriptor. What did my 12-year-old mind create as a story? My mind developed the narrative that I had no talent in music, I was not athletic and I was not beautiful. Sure, I was "smart" but, that wasn't as exciting as the other descriptions used on my siblings.

Throughout many conversations in my teen years, we were compared. One that stood out to me is the notion that a person needed more than being smart to succeed since, "the world opens for beautiful people". My mind completed the phrase with, "... like my sister". I created an entire foundation of insecurities based on my comparisons to my older siblings. Please note, these comparisons were not meant to hurt anyone. They were truthful observations. The comments weren't meant to degrade one over the other. Somehow, my mind created a story that if those attributes described my siblings, they were not meant for me. Think back to your childhood. Did you do the same? Did you interpret a compliment for another as a detriment to yourself?

When I became an older teen, as typical, I compared myself to my peers and to the women I saw in movies, television and even toys. It was my custom to watch who was considered beautiful, popular, and what was trending. This was a strange and confusing time for me. I was a teen in the 1980s. Big hair, feathered bangs, being blonde and leggy was the trend. I had the big Chaka Khan hair. That was as close to the popular image I achieved. The popular dolls were blonde bombshells of which were unachievable for a short, French-Creole/Filipina. Would there be no reprieve from my observations of lack?

I did have several saving graces regarding beauty. My Mother, Grandmother and Aunties. They were definitely not blonde bombshells. To me, they are the most beautiful women in the world. In my young mind, I added a stipulation that my mother's family were an exception of which I was not part of.

I diligently added to my bricks of insecurities.

When I applied for college, I hit new obstacles. Remember, the talent that distinguished me from my siblings is that I am smart. Going to college should be a fantastic experience for me. It wasn't. I would build such anxiety over tests that even though I knew the information, knowing I was going to be graded would cause my brain to freeze. The college entrance exams were torture for me. Test anxiety was crippling. I was smart. That's all I had, and the only way to prove it was through tests that would cause me panic attacks. It was a double-edged sword.

Somehow, despite my test anxiety, I was accepted into some rather prestigious universities and offered a few scholarships. In a perfect world, this would be exciting news. Unfortunately, I was told that men needed jobs to provide for the families and a woman's place was to support the man. If I accepted a scholarship at a prestigious school, I would prevent a young man from attending. He needed that seat more than I would. Why would I need a degree if I would end up barefoot and pregnant? I would waste precious money and time.

With that mentality seeded into my mind, I declined all offers with the exception of one. I attended the University of Nebraska to pursue an Engineering degree. During the first week of classes, I was kicked out of my parent's home to fend for myself. It was a huge misunderstanding that I wasn't given the opportunity to explain. It was a difficult time for me since I was underage and unable to sign documents to lease an apartment or purchase a car. My saving grace, was meeting a fellow student, who is still a very close friend, who took me under her wing, provided shelter and transportation to help me get my bearings to survive.

To become more self-sufficient, I juggled full-time school with three part-time jobs and one weekend job. This sounds more difficult than it was. I was young and determined to prove my worth. Speaking of worth, do you think being kicked out of my parental home messed with my perception of worth? It most certainly did! I cried myself to sleep whenever I had time before I passed out between jobs. I had friends around me, but I was too busy working and attending school to spend time with any of them. I kept my nose to the grindstone to simply survive on a daily basis.

It was about a year after I was on my own when I diverted from my routine. While at my weekend job as a server at a restaurant, the other servers asked if we could have a small gathering at my studio apartment. We were all the same age, but I was the only one who didn't live with my parents. I agreed with the caveat that everyone must leave by one AM because I had to sleep before I needed to drive to my other job. After our shift at the restaurant was over, we met at my apartment to play board games and unwind.

We were all having a good time when one of the servers said he invited the new boy to join us. He was from out of town and didn't know many people. There was a knock at the door and the new boy enters. He seemed nice enough. We all had a good time together. It came to one AM and everyone left as planned. I got ready for bed and had the small 20-inch television on. I hadn't unfolded my sofa-bed out to retire for the evening, when there was knock at the door. I looked out the peep hole and saw the new boy at my door.

Me: "Everyone is gone."

Him: "I forgot my jacket in your closet.'

I looked in the closet and didn't see a jacket.

Me: "There isn't a jacket."

Him: "I put it on the shelf."

I stepped away from the closet and sure enough, well out of my reach was a black leather jacket.

I was far too short to reach the jacket and I didn't have a chair to retrieve it, so I opened the door. He strolled in, got his jacket and jumped over the back of my sofa bed and sat to watch television.

Me: "You need to leave."

Him: "What would you say if you saw me on television?" (There was a police show playing showing suspects in crimes.)

Me: "I'd act like I didn't see you."

Him: "Damn straight you would."

He proceeded to pull a gun from his jacket, pointed it at me and ordered me to sit next to him. He moved in and kept me as his captive victim for over 10 months. In public, he was the life of the party and everyone kept telling me I was so lucky to have someone who loved me. In private, he was a monster. All my self-doubt had me wondering if this was the only love I was worthy of. Even when I called the police, they said this was just a lover's quarrel and refused to get involved. I believed my life and the lives of everyone who knew me, were in danger. He threatened if I ever told what he was doing, he would slaughter whomever I told, while I was forced to watch. It would be my fault.

I share this tiny bit of my story because while I was repeatedly attacked by this boy, all my insecurities, my inner-critics and every negative comment I every allowed into my mind boiled back up as confirmation of why he was doing what he was.

annoying

ridiculous

idiot

stupid
fat
short
slow
gangly
awkward
tramp
scrawny
ugly
useless
lazy
no good
not good enough
waste of time
hate you
no one wants you
Wish you were never BORN!

I justified his actions toward me with my own insecurities. Words are powerful. Be careful how you use them and how you perceive them. Did you harshly judge yourself? Do you still? How heavy is the weight of your insecurities? What are you not permitting yourself to do?

My heart was blocked from love and acceptance of the authentic version of me. It took years of intentional inner work to overcome the mountain of self-doubt and the mental prison I built around me. Even after I got away, I was afraid that success would lead to recognition, and recognition would lead my attacker back to me. I had to break through all those mindsets. I am living proof that escape from our prisons is possible, the secret is… we hold our own key. Choose to live fully present.

Why are you playing small? It's time to give yourself permission to be the best version of you every day. Stop apologizing for what you lack, step into who you are, and Live Unapologetically!

MICHELLE MRAS

Michelle is a survivor of multiple life challenges to include a Traumatic Brain Injury and Breast Cancer. She guides others to recognize the innate gifts within them, stop apologizing for what they are not and step into who they truly are.

She accomplishes this through one-on-one and group coaching, Training events, Keynote talks, her books, and Podcasts.

Michelle has been awarded the Inspirational Women of Excellence Award from the Women Economic Forum, New Delhi, India; the John Maxwell Team Culture Award for Positive Attitude; has speaking parts in a few SyFy movies check the IMDB.com database for her. She has been featured on hundreds of Podcasts, radio programs, several magazines, quoted in books and has a habit of breaking out into song. Her books: 1) Eat, Drink and Be Mary - A glimpse into a life well lived, 2) It's Not Luck - Overcoming you, 3) 13 Steps to Riches - Desire

Michelle's driving thought is that every day is a gift. Tomorrow is never promised. Every moment is an opportunity to be the best version of you… Unapologetically!

International TEDx Speaker, Communication Trainer, Speaker Coach, Co-Host of the Denim & Pearls podcast, the Author of Eat, Drink and Be Mary: A Glimpse Into a Life Well Lived and It's Not Luck: Overcoming You. Michelle is the Host of the MentalShift show on The New Channel (TNC), Philippines.

Denim & Pearls podcast http://bit.ly/3gYHBzu

https://www.youtube.com/playlist?list=PLAkbmMOlqev0CbVMleqlJMIT0HS_uHMLF

www.YouTube.com/MichelleMras

www.YouTube.com/MichelleMras

Me@Michellemras.com

www.MichelleMras.com

CHAPTER 8

Provision not Punishment

Mindy East

Just like that, I was left at the curb.

My husband didn't even pull into the driveway before letting me out of his truck. He stopped in the street in front of our house, told me he had filed for divorce and that I would be served papers sometime the next day, and just like that, he drove out of my world. Thirty five years of marriage ended in the gutter on a Monday evening in early June 2013.

I had felt this pain before. Over the past decade as he had pulled me through chaos infested waters like a skier behind a speed boat in an ocean full of sharks and predators. The marriage had been on life support since he had been caught having an affair with one of his employees years before. Once again the familiar pain creeping into my stomach, was back. It had been been my constant companion over the years, causing me to lose weight, lose sleep, and lose confidence.

We had been separated off and on four years over the past decade and from the outside looking in, were the perfect power couple; high school sweethearts, three beautiful kids, business owners. We lived in an executive residence behind a brick wall, with wrought iron gates and security cameras on a large recreational lake. We lived a big life with a big house and big problems. In reality we only had the power to wreck our world and no power to fix it.

We fought to stay together…well one of us did. I was the patient, long suffering wife who held down the fort, managed the kids, the house and property, while he sat on the fence, ran his business, or traveled with his mistress. I put my trust in God, spending all my waking time praying that He would soften my husband's heart and turn it towards home. Our kids were teens when the affair had first become public and he moved out of the house. We had one in college, one in high school and one in middle school. My heart was always set on healing and reconciliation so I resisted the temptation to trash his name or reputation to our children, family and friends. I told our kids, "Right or wrong, he is still your dad and you need to respect him." He wasn't a bad person; he just got very lost somewhere along the way, so we sold the big house and built a beautiful new one. At one time I was more attached to the house than I was the husband, but it was ultimately my idea to get out from under the stress and besides, I always wondered if "she" had been in my house when I was away with the kids attending a wedding.

It seemed to work for a while as we settled into our new home together in 2009. I started a new job, he sold his company, we got completely out of debt as the kids grew up. I hoped the new changes in our lives would give us a fresh, clean start, but soon he became increasingly distant and started spending more and more time away from us as his obsession going to the gym daily for hours ramped up. I suspected he had dabbled in the use of steroids, as this had been a way for him to focus on his bodybuilding and to burn off his stress, but it also brought new temptation into his life and soon he slipped into another affair with a woman 17 years his junior who he got pregnant in the fall of 2012.

He chose to tell me the bad news at bedtime the night before I was to leave on a 4-day business trip. We stayed up until 1:30 am as he tried to convince me she was unstable and had pursued him. I left our house at 5:30 am to catch my flight and they terminated the pregnancy later that same day.

I was sick. I told him that was not okay with me, but it was too late for me to save an innocent life.

I settled into a routine of numbness of just going through the motions of trying to be my best as a mother, but my heart grew hard at the thought of trying to be a wife to him and all intimacy was gone. I still took care of him, and the two kids who were now in college, doing all the cooking and cleaning and managing the house, but that wall around my heart grew dark and hard. My belief in God keep me in the marriage, but I told my husband I could not walk this path with him again. He apologized profusely and told me their affair was over. He argued that she was a raging alcoholic with a pacemaker due to past substance abuse and mentally unstable.

So I stayed.

I trudged on through the holidays, into the New Year, but I was lost, alone, lonely and miserable. I didn't share my secret with anyone. I was still trusting God and I didn't want to leave a legacy of divorce to my children, so I put God first, my kids second, my husband third, and myself last. I was embarrassed, ashamed and my heart was shattered. I was a dark place for the next six months.

The end of May we took a trip to Mexico with our family and friends, but my husband was distant and detached through out the week, especially towards me. One evening, after dinner he was away from our group talking on his phone when our son overheard a woman's voice on the other end. He quickly told me, but since we were with a group, I told him I would handle the matter later. I still remember the look on his face. He was a freshman in college and a 6'2 football player but at that moment, but he looked like a scared little boy not knowing what to do next.

Two days after our return, my husband made a surprise announcement that he was going to LA to check into a business opportunity. While he was gone, I came to the conclusion that he was involved with someone else, and it was confirmed to me when he was silent for 4 days. I sat at home and prayed, but I had a deep sense of foreboding I couldn't shake.

"You take care of the earth and water it, making it rich and fertile. The rivers of God will not run dry, they provide a bountiful harvest of grain, for You have ordered it so." ~ Psalm 65:9

How often did I see dark clouds forming on the horizon and fear the coming storm?

What if the winds of change blew in the direction of my house? My family? My marriage? What if hail and wind, lightning and thunder threatened all I have built? What if an F-5 tornado leveled a path of destruction wiping out all that I held near and dear? What if God sent the storm to clear a path for something new that He wanted to do in my life?

God orders and He delivers. When my steps are established by Him, I am right where I need to be; covered with a mantle of abundance, blessings and prosperity. We must accept and believe the storm is necessary to take care of us and provide weather in our lives for that which needs the encouragement to grow, blossom and flourish.

We must not fear the coming storm - since God ordered it, it's power can only do so much damage before He uses it to bring new life and growth.

I walked into the house as he drove away and I was met by my two youngest kids, and I told them matter of factly what was happening. Our world had been full of fun, travel, expensive toys, hobbies, fancy cars and houses, and now none of that mattered. None of it.

I called my dad, my two best friends and tried to process what was happening. Within 30 minutes, I had 6 close friends show up and we cried together. My next door neighbor had recently lost her son in an accident while he was away at college, and she recognized the signs of a family emergency when multiple cars pulled up and people rushed inside. She told me later that when she looked inside my house all the lights were on and everyone was standing up in the living room.

"People stand when it's bad news" she said.

The blur of the next few days turned into weeks and I cried that whole summer. Not for what I had lost, but for what I should have had. What I could have had. He was back with the much younger woman whom he got pregnant and had a drinking problem, and moved across the country to a beach community in California. In some ways the process of being divorced was easier than I expected as it methodically played out, but in other ways it was brutal as we began the process of dividing the contents of our house that defined our lifetime together. Heartbreak is too gentle of a word to describe the pain of stripping away all our possessions and having to sell the marital home and all the things that had meant so much to me as we were raising our children. Dividing up the family albums and our kids baby books was devastating, but I had to be the strong and stable parent for our kids since he had left. He came back to town for the closing, packed up his belongings, and left again.

In the end, all that was left were some crumbs and papers as I closed the door on our beautiful family home and all it represented and that chapter of my life.

My faith in God grew stronger with each passing day and by early fall I was able to see things from a different perspective. At first I thought of the divorce as a punishment but then I saw it as a provision. While I was married, I had tried and cried, preached and prayed, but nothing I did was effective at changing my spouse or making him love me. We didn't fight, we didn't really discuss anything either. We even spent 3 years in Christian marital counseling at our church, but he had no desire to put any effort into rebuilding our marriage. We had friends come along side of us who tried their best to lift and encourage us on, and even a couple from our church tried to mentor us into a better relationship, but in the end he wanted out, so he left.

At night when the house was quiet, my mind raced.I used to wonder, "Why wasn't I enough?"

He was a bodybuilder, who spent time every day working out, tanning and doing cardio in the gym. He noticed other's personal appearances, so naturally he was critical of my weight. But I was pretty, wasn't I? I dressed up with heels and makeup, I was into health and wellness, but not to the extent that he was. The fact that I was slim and attractive made it even more confusing to me, and others on the outside looking in, but then I realized something liberating during my journey.

It's not that I wasn't enough. It's that I was too much.

Too strong. Too brave. Too bold. Too beautiful. Too sexy. I was too much of something that made him feel less than. It was also my energy… It asked him to rise up to become the best possible version of himself. But not everyone is willing to go where they would grow, so he felt pressured and withdrew from me. During the divorce I asked him,

"Honey, what happened to us?"

"I never felt good enough." he replied.

"But why? I never made you feel that way."

He looked at me with a blank stare as if he was trying to come up with an answer that never did.

This was very eye opening to me. It was at that time I realized that having an affair has very little to do with the wife or the other woman, but it has everything to do with that person and how he feels about himself.

Counseling gave me some insight into the behaviors and feelings that occur in adults from suffering adverse childhood experiences. Psychological trauma, neglect, feelings of abandonment, physical and emotional abuse and anger inside the home can all attribute to problems that stem from childhood and show up during the adult years as dependencies, mental issues and as myriad of coping skills trying to numb the pain that was never addressed.

My husband grew up with an angry and overbearing father who was verbally and physically abusive. He shared in counseling that one time he came home from grade school with a fat lip as a result of a scuffle on the playground with another boy. Upon entering the house, his dad bellowed at him to get into the truck. "Either you kick his ass or I'll kick yours!"

My husband as a little boy sat bleeding and scared until they pulled up in front of the house where the other boy lived. He walked up the front porch, pounded on the screen door until his classmate opened the door. He glanced over his shoulder and at that moment his only safe choice was to take his chances with the little kid again over his fathers rage. It made me cry to think that the very man who is supposed to love and protect him as a small child was threatening to hurt him instead. It's no wonder he had issues as an adult.

As we had tried to repair the marriage, the subject of trust was discussed frequently. I was pouring salt into a wound every time I would question his whereabouts or ask why he had not returned my calls. Trust is like writing a book; it takes a long time to write the words, but a book burns instantly when thrown into a fire. To me, it was his job for me to trust him; it was my job to forgive, but I represented the mortgage, the kids, the bills, the responsibilities. The other women he got involved with were his way of escaping his life. His business had been affected profoundly after 911 and he had some financial pressures as a result of owning a large company that was hit hard during the recession. He became moody, sullen and distracted.

Some women are predatory women. They pick out a man, and

it doesn't matter if he has a wife and family at home, it becomes a competition to them to try to lure him away as a prize to fluff up their own ego. When my husband turned 40, his employees honored him with a surprise party and my mother pulled me aside with an ominous warning,

"Be careful. It's not the beautiful flamingo, or colorful peacock who tries to steal your nest out from under you; it's the little brown wren."

All the conditions were right. He was handsome, successful and powerful. Both of the women he got involved with were predatory women who wanted my lifestyle. They couldn't earn it legitimately so they had to steal mine from me. They both had less advantages than me growing up and did not come from a loving home like I did. Plus they had issues.

One day when I was particularly sad, I saw a photo that spoke to me. It was a hot air ballon rising up into the air with a person hanging on to a rope about a dozen feet off the ground, with the caption that read "Let go or get dragged."

I got dragged a lot of years.

The process of getting divorced lasted longer than his relationship with the girl at the beach and he was back in our hometown after 7 months. He wanted to reconcile, and stop the divorce proceedings, but by that point, I was not interested. He again apologized, saying 'I'm sorry I ruined your life" and I said " You didn't ruin my life; you set me free."

When I turned him down, he quickly took up again with the former employee and they got married in a matter of a few months. Now, I had to do my work on forgiving her all over again. I have never gotten an apology for the pain she caused me and my children but for my sake I knew I had to get past the hurt in my heart and find a way, otherwise I would be trapped in the past.

I have been a believer since I was a child, so when this happened

I invited God into my situation. Over the years I had asked Him to heal and restore my marriage, when that didn't happen I realized He was going to heal and restore me instead. My prayer went from, "Change him Lord" to "Change me instead." I was raised in the church, but even as a young bride at age 19, I didn't fully comprehend having God involved in our marriage. I never consulted Him, so why would He be obligated to restore a marriage that didn't center around or involve Him? I had always wanted my husband to be the spiritual leader of our marriage and family, but he was reluctant, so I promoted myself by default. I made sure the kids were raised as Christians, attending church, VBS and had a spiritual background, but ultimately, my shoulders were never built to carry that load and my husband ended up resenting my attempts to promote myself into that role.

I had a lot of experience in practicing forgiveness but once I thought I had gotten past something, it reared it's ugly head again so I had to dig down deeper to get to the root. Now I had to allow my emotions to catch up to his decision, so I pictured his new wife as a little girl. I knew she had not been raised in the loving home like me with all the advantages that I had. I knew she too had issues in her background coming from a large lower middle class family and she had a failed first marriage where her husband had been abusive with her. Maybe it wasn't compatibility or love that brought them back together as much as it was the psychological wounds they both shared.

In the book of Genesis, Abraham is standing in his tent when God lead him outside to look up at the sky and count the stars, it was then that God made a covenant with him to be the "Father of Many Nations" and the promise extended to bless his dependents as well.

After the divorce was final, I flew to New York City to attend an event when I had my own Abraham moment with God. It was on that trip that I was introduced to the positive and motivational leadership of a keynote speaker who spoke my same language. He reintroduced me to the scripture "As a man thinks in his heart, so he is" from Proverbs 23:7 and from the book by James Allen. I had been so busy living my life trying to make, or keep my ex-husband happy, that I hadn't set any goals or discovered any dreams for myself. God had to take me out of my house and into the business capital of the world with all it's energy, glitter and lights to give me my own promise. What I could see by faith, He would give to me!

I came back home with a new, fresh perspective and creative energy flowing through my mind and in my thoughts. I had been in the Marketing Director for the nation's extreme weather expert and a life long weather enthusiast. I have lived in Tornado Alley all my life and the Midwest is perfect for the development of some of the most massive storms of our lifetime. A pop up thunderstorm was a common occurrence during the summer months and if the cool air that rises up over the Rockies mixes with the warm winds that blow up from the Gulf and become organized into rotation, a tornado could occur. I always had a fascination with weather since I was a teenager and owned two horses. I kept them at a stable 4 miles away from my house so I would ride everyday after school along the river or past the plentiful fields of wheat that Kansas is famous for. It was at that time I noticed the effects weather had on animals; the rise and fall of the barometric pressure is a trigger for changes in their disposition and behavior. It could be bright, warm and sunny outside and they would be hard to handle or extra frisky, and sure enough, a thunderstorm would roll through the area later that night.

While attending some of the large scale weather events across the country, I realized children either loved the weather or were afraid of it. I believe in Divine inspiration, and the idea to write a kids weather book seemed to just download into my brain based on my experience growing up. In 2014 I wrote and published my first book ,The Animals' Weather

Guide for Children using animal's instinctive behaviors to educate and empower the young reader to stay safe in any weather event that might arise. The next year I wrote The Animals' Guide to Weather Around the World and Other Natural Wonders. I also resigned from my position as Marketing Director and started my own speaker's agency signing my former boss as my first client as I continued to trust God to establish the order of my steps.

Three years after the divorce, I had become disenchanted with dating in my fifties. I seemed to be attracted to and attracting the same type of men as my ex husband, so I had a come to Jesus meeting with God and told Him I wanted Him to choose a man for me. I took myself off the market, took the limits off of God and waited for Him to make His presentation. I know that God always gives His best to those who leave the choice with Him, and my prayers were sent up into the Heavenly realm where they mixed with the prayers of a former class mate living 1400 miles away who was believing the same for his life. He had been single for 17 years living in LA, but we attended the same high school together and our families were long time friends. Our friendship grew over the course of many months with emails, phone calls and texts. He wrote me beautiful love letters, and captivated me with his tenderness. After a year while he got to know my heart, mind and soul, he crossed a mountain range to propose to me and we celebrated our engagement surrounded by our children and family. In the fall of 2017 were joined in marriage witnessed by God, our family and friends four years after the divorce.

Now that my ex-husband and I had each remarried, we had to settle on the business of coming together as co-parents to celebrate our children and grandchildren. We had many happy occasions to celebrate as a family including engagements, marriages, baby showers, reveal parties, births, and birthdays. My ex-husband had been such an integral part of our lives so we settled into a good working relationship where I applied myself to coexist peacefully for my sake and the sake of our family. I had to accept the divorce, salvage the best, and forgive the rest. I knew that forgiveness did not change the past; it changed the future and I could not reach my dreams and goals if I spent that energy on hate and strife. Yes, I had prayed and prayed for God to heal my marriage, and that didn't happen, but I always trusted Him and kept doing good, so if I did fall short, at least I was falling forward and He would honor my effort. God always gives you what you ask for or, something better. I was experiencing better in a wonderful Godly marriage to a Godly man, and my personal life and career were both reaching new heights, but I still had one final test to pass.

The first time I had to be in their home together brought up a flood of emotions I wasn't ready to handle.

We were celebrating one of our kid's birthdays and as I looked around their house, I saw all the material possessions that used to be in my house; the art we picked out together now hung on her wall. The bookcase I had displayed my childhood books and trinkets in now showcased her favorites instead of mine. The sculpture I gave to my husband for our anniversary, now had a place of prominence in her living room. I know they were just "things" but those "things" used to belong to me. Just like he used to.

"How dare she?" This woman had entered into an affair with a married man, with children still living at home, and her boss no less. I got through the evening okay but a dark mood followed me home and stayed with me for several days. I felt ashamed to be attached to material things, but they represented the emotions of a painful event in my life that was still affecting me.

In my mind, I kept reliving all the personal offenses I had taken and soon I had built up enough righteous energy to fuel a large section of a thriving metropolis. I thought I could handle this as a solo committee member. I was the case manager, project manager and quality control all rolled into one, but I was failing miserably.

Judgement and hurt feelings threatened to take up residence in my heart closing up a wall and blocking out the light. It was beginning to consume me. It got so bad that I had to do something other than wallow in my self-inflicted misery. So I reached out to Upper Management.

When I finally called the support desk upstairs, God was quick to get back with me. His instructions were for me to read the story of Sodom and Gomorrah.

"Lord? What does the story of Sodom and Gomorrah have to do with this situation, besides the obvious?" I asked.

He told me to go read the passage for my marching orders. "Oh great! another battle. Why does everything have to be so hard?' I thought. However, I knew it was for my own good so I rushed to open my Bible and found the perfect answer to soothe my dark and wounded heart.

In Genesis 19:17, two angels came to Lot's door and grabbed his hands along with his family and escorted them outside the city.

"Escape for your life! Do not look behind you or stop anywhere in the whole valley; escape to the mountains, lest you be consumed."

So, that's it? That's all?

It was so simple. I wasn't going in that direction any longer. We had already divided our belongings when we parted ways, and I had recently been married to the Godly man of my dreams. My life and career were soaring, so why was I getting hung up on the past when my present and future were so bright and happy? I had been looking so closely at what I had lost instead of what I had gained that I needed to step back to look at my life through a different lens.

What I heard Him say to me was; "Remove yourself. Don't watch, don't obsess, don't look back, keep going higher and rise above this. Keep moving forward...Their part in your story is over. Let them go and keep moving because they can't go where I am taking you next."

They represented my past. His future for me was out up in front of me, and was so much bigger than anything I had given up or had left behind. In covenant, we offer God what we have, and in exchange He gives us what He has. I gave Him my heart block, my weaknesses, my failures, my hurt feelings, my disappointments, my raw emotions, and He gave me His strength, His grace, His love and His peace that passes all understanding. He gave me beauty for ashes. One of my favorite scriptures is Galatians 6:9. "Do not grow weary in doing good, for at the proper time you will reap a harvest if you do not give up."Not just enough for a sandwich or a loaf of bread, but a harvest! More than enough to share with others.

My present and my future are so blessed and the pain and hurt have been replaced with a peace and calm that has carried into my life with others. My company, Baron Ridge Speakers Agency, has grown from 1 to 24 professional keynote speakers and event emcees from across the country and one from Africa, I have been featured in magazines, interviewed on podcasts, spoken before others and I have recently been named the host of a new television show, Ageless Enthusiasm, coming out this fall. Isn't that the best happy ending I could ever write? Well, it was actually God's idea, so to Him goes all the Glory...Especially for the ones that involve the heart.

MINDY EAST

Owner of Baron Ridge Speakers Agency representing 24 professional keynote speakers and event emcees from across the nation, including one in Africa. Upcoming host of Ageless Enthusiasm~It's an Attitude on PBS KANSAS, redefining life, health and happiness over 50! Happily married to Mark East with 3 adult kids, 3 bonus kids, and 8 grandchildren. Author of The Animals' Weather Guide for Children (2014), and The Animals' Guide to Weather Around the World and Other Natural Wonders. (2015)

https://baronridgeproductions.com/

CHAPTER 9

Dichotomy

C. Regi Rodgers

What is a dichotomy? This word is a word that is seldom heard but it has such a diverse yet difficult meaning. When I think of this word it brings to my mind a tailspin. As if someone is stuck chasing their tail. What does this word actually mean? The word dichotomy means, a division or contrast between two things that are or are represented as being opposed or entirely different.

The Greek word for this is "Dikhotomia", it means in two, apart.

A dichotomy is a contrast between two things, especially two opposed ideas, like war and peaceor love and hate. Sometimes in life we find ourselves in a dichotomy. This is a very crucial and complicated space to be in. We find ourselves dealing with two opposing entities. There is a scripture that says, "Every time I want to do right, wrong is always present." This is the epitome of a dichotomy. This almost sounds like a juxtaposition.

What is the difference between dichotomy and juxtaposition? A dichotomy is a separation or division into two; a distinction that results in such a division while a juxtaposition is the nearness of objects with no delimiter.

In the anthropological field of theology and in philosophy, dichotomy is the belief that humans consist of a soul and a body. This stands in stark contrast to trichotomy. There are some who believe that we are tripartite or trichotomist. This represents body, soul, and spirit. Whether we believe in humans being dichotomist or trichotomist is irrelevant. Both have entities that need to be in agreement. Because a house (body) divided against itself cannot stand. There are three rooms in this one house (body) for some, and there are two rooms in this house (body) for others. The mind-body problem is a debate concerning the relationship between thought and consciousness in the human mind, and the brain as part of the physical body.

I think this helps to shed more light when you hear someone say, "your heart says one thing and the mind says another." This creates a heart block. The heart pumps blood. Blood is needed for survival. The heart does not have components that manifest as thinking and feeling. The brain allows us to think, feel, and act. The brain is what creates the emotions and thoughts. The heart merely supplies blood to the brain and the rest of the body. The heart keeps the brain alive using the blood. Emotions causes changes in our heart rate. Changes in our heart rate affect our emotions too. This dichotomy becomes magnified because of what we are dealing with and these heart blocks become very apparent. Now you feel as if you are torn between your heart and your mind.

I'm so honored to be one of the authors in this book. I have experienced this in my life. I have been torn between my heart and my mind. This caused me to react and behave with my heart instead of my mind. It created a heart block. What is a heart block? When a signal is slowed down or kept from sending it's message, this then becomes a heart block.

My father the late Rev. Boyd E. Rodgers died in an automobile accident in 2000. He actually had a heart attack while driving and ran into the back of a cargo truck in Philadelphia, in front of the Art Museum. He was my hero, my buddy, my mentor and now he's gone. My parents had 5 boys, I was the youngest of the 5. My father was a good man. Im sure most children feel this about their father. I can honestly say, I have never seen my father drink any alcohol, smoke a cigarette, nor do any drugs. My father was a beloved father, pastor of thousands, and a devoted husband. His untimely death put me in a tailspin which gave me a heart block. I was in a dichotomy and didn't know what to do or how to feel. It would appear as if my world stopped and my life was changed and would never be the same.

I had never experienced the feelings that are attached to losing a loved one. I was surprised by the range of emotions that I experienced. I didn't know what grief would feel like. The death of my dad was a devastating experience. The loss and pain that I felt struck me very deeply. It felt like I was being cut in two. I felt like I had lost a part of me. I know that it's natural and normal to grieve when someone we love dies, but I don't think that we are ever really ready for it. There is no right way to grieve, everyone reacts in their own way. This shock made me numb, it's hard to believe that the person I loved dearly, the man who taught me how to be a man, the man who sat me down and gave me pearls of wisdom is not coming back. I felt disorientated, I felt like I lost my place and purpose in life. Feelings of pain and distress following bereavement can be overwhelming and very frightening.

There are multiple layers of heart blocks that surface: Anger, Guilt, Depression, Physical Health Issues, A Sense of Longing and Belonging.

The truth is, healing comes at a slow pace. But it does eventually come. No one will ever replace my father, but I recognized and realized that I was able to gradually continue life and overcome the Heart Blocks. Although there was a loss, I actually gained. My dad had his accident in Sept. 2000 and I moved to Las Vegas from Philadelphia in Sept. 2001. I set out keep my dad's legacy in tact and to start a whole new journey. This pushed me to write my first book entitled "Playa2Praya." I dedicated it to my dad. I felt like he was pushing me even tho he was no longer here on earth as I knew him to be. Yet he was with me. I have been able to garner some success in Las Vegas and nationally. I am a radio host, television host, podcast host and as I've already shared an author. I write a full page column for the #1 magazine in Las Vegas. I constantly feel my dad with me, just as I constantly have feelings of him not being here physically anymore. This dichotomy is beginning to make sense.

Dichotomies represent two opposing forces that create a conflict. It is the clear delineation of the protagonist versus the antagonist. Whether it's external or internal. This gave me a clear understanding as to why heart blocks formed, two opposing forces. Dichotomies are essential I believe because this is what allows us to actually overcome the heart blocks. At some point we modify our mindset, we adjust our attitude, we maneuver our mentality. Dealing with death, particularly a loved one, is one the most stressful experience that you can go through. Everyone reacts differently to death, and it's normal if you feel like your riding on a rollercoaster of different emotions.

Sadness is a basic part of life. Sometimes we struggle with how to deal with being sad. The first thing that I suggest to you is to pause. Don't act on your feelings right away. Take some time to recalibrate. The second thing that I suggest is to acknowledge what you feel. Whatever it is that your feeling, it is alright to feel like that. The third thing that I suggest is to think. Think about what it is going to take to make yourself feel better. Some people like to vent. Venting is taking an opportunity to share your feelings out loud. We do this naturally when we talk to someone that we trust. Do not suppress your sadness and pretend that it does not exist. Ignoring what you are feeling is not the thing that I suggest anyone should do. This does not make what your feeling go away. This can cause what your feeling to come out in different ways causing more heart blocks. Our emotions act as signals to show us that what we are doing in our life is or isn't working. Feelings can be a signal that something needs to change. If we don't change the situations or thought patterns that are causing the uncomfortable emotions, we will continue to allow the heart blocks to build.

We have to keep in mind that those heart blocks can be removed and that we will overcome. We cannot allow the stress to affect us physically nor emotionally. We can eliminate these heart blocks one block at a time. It's important to take some time to recover and relax. When you feel like things are building up, talk to someone you trust. We don't have to cope with this alone. While death is inevitable, our emotional responses and reactions to it vary dramatically. There are no scripts about how to cope with a loss or how long it will take to remove the heart blocks.

Everyone reacts to a loss at their own pace. Everyone who copes with a loss of a loved one share a range of common emotions and feelings, all of this is normal. Don't feel ashamed about how you feel. If you feel like crying, by all means cry. Use crying as a cure. At some point you will wipe those tears away. Those tears will eventually dry up. The true dichotomy is, you might be crying today, tomorrow you may be laughing. Weeping may endure for a night, but joy comes in the morning. Hang on and hang in there!

C. REGI RODGERS

Through years of counseling countless couples, C. Regi Rodgers brings a provocative conversation anytime he is called upon to speak or do an interview. Formerly celebrated as a Pastor, he also authored an internet column entitled " Rev. Regi's Recess" which appeared in the Gospel EUR. Venturing to

Las Vegas from Philadelphia, the city of "Brotherly Love and Sisterly Affection" to Sin City to begin anew after the sudden loss of his father in a car accident in late 2000.

Regi also released his first book and CD titled "PLAYA 2 PRAYA" that same year which he dedicated to his late father. This author is a keen observer of the relationship field, the space where people come out to play. Some play fair, many with hidden agenda's, most without skill or clarity. He has appeared as a guest on TCT Network "I'm Just Saying", Wynn Network "The John Wynn Show", The Word Network "Heavenly Sent", TV57 in Atlanta on Atlanta Live, The Mother Love Show, The Tamron Hall Show, IHeart Radio with "Art Chat Daddy Sims", and other local cable and national radio programming as well. He was also featured in "ENCORE" Magazine. HE is a contributing writer for the #1 Magazine in Las Vegas "MyVegas" Magazine where he writes a full page column on "Dating and Relationships." He is a radio host on 87.9Heat Fm Charlotte, his show is called "REGI'S RECESS" Real talk Real relationships! It airs every Wednesday evening 9pm est. He also has a Podcast entitled " REGI'S RECESS" Real talk Real relationships! This is live streamed every Wednesday on Facebook Live. His latest book is entitled "LOVE AT FIRST SPIRIT", this also comes with a workbook which is a 21 day challenge for ladies. One is the Ying and one is the Yang. People call him a relationship guru and he is known as the #1 Relationship Coach who gives "Dating From An Expanded Conscious Perspective." He is evolutionary and revolutionary. He provides Real talk about Real relationships that expands into contemporary mainstream consciousness.

He will be releasing a new book on Dating and Relationships!

CHAPTER 10

From a Vortex of Death to a Victory of Spirit
An Unlikely Trip that Saved My Soul

Kellan Fluckiger

Crescendo

When the crashing and the banging and screeching stopped, and the dust settled, I slowly exhaled and opened my eyes.

One-quarter inch in front of my left eyeball was a tree branch about a half-inch in diameter. It slowly dawned on me that a couple of inches more would have made me look like an extra in a bad horror movie.

I looked at my 14-year-old son, who was over in the passenger seat. Miraculously, he also seemed to be okay. We looked at each other for a moment and took in the gravity of the situation.

We had the top down on the convertible, so I slowly extricated myself from the driver's side. My son got out, and we stood together surveying the situation. We were blessed because the car had not rolled over. Unfortunately, the wood and metal fence was trashed for at least 20 m, and we had smashed into a giant tree which was just on the other side of the fence line.

It was a Sunday morning. We stood for a few moments with not a soul was in sight. After a few minutes, we heard sirens and knew someone was probably on the way. Obviously, someone had heard or seen something, but we hadn't seen anyone.

My mind was racing, and I was trying to figure out what to do. What my son did not know was that I was high on cocaine and some other substances. The last thing in the world I wanted was ambulances, police, and blood tests.

It was a single-car accident, so there were no witnesses except us. My fear and my shame were of equal proportions. I choked back panic, rage, and self-loathing in equal proportions. I had no business driving in this condition.

The 850 hp convertible supercar we had been driving was trashed beyond hope. It was an utter miracle that either one of us was still breathing.

Soon enough, the ambulance arrived, with the police and the fire truck shortly thereafter. What happened next will stick in my memory forever. The emergency services personnel were looking around for corpses they were sure had been killed in the crash.

They assumed my son and me, who were un-scratched, were simply bystanders who were rubbernecking on the scene. Finally, I said to one of the medics, "This was my car, and I was driving." He took one look at the destruction and particularly noted the driving compartment, and shook his head.

"That's impossible." "You can't have been in that driver's compartment."

"Well, I was driving, and this is my son, and he was the passenger." "We are both okay and don't really need anything."

"You need to go to the hospital to get checked out."

"I'm fine, and I don't want to go anywhere." The last thing in the world I needed was to get a blood test and then get arrested.

I was single again, for the third time, living with four teenage children. Getting thrown in jail would not do well. Besides, I had a high-profile job, and the scandal would be horrific.

After some back-and-forth, we were told we had to sign a document that demonstrated we had been offered hospital care and refused.

My son didn't say anything; he just wanted to get out of there. As soon as they would allow it, I sent him away from the scene. He walked home, which is what I asked him to do. He waited for me there.

After more conversation, I too walked away from the scene and never spoke of the incident again except to my son, who had been involved. He probably suspected something was wrong, but nothing was ever said.

As I walked home, I was sick to my stomach. Depression, self-loathing, rage, and a small dose of undeserved relief were mixed in wild proportions in my heart.

Insurance handled everything, and I received a large check several weeks later as settlement for the totaled hot rod.

This was simply another in a long series of failures in my life.

Just weeks before that incident, one of my daughters commented that they all expected one day to either find me dead or get news that I had died in some sort of accident. My comment deflected the gravity of her worry.

I simply said, "yes, that's probably true."

How in the world did I get to such a desperate and low level in my life?

The Start of It All

The discipline applied in my upbringing, all the way till I graduated high school, would be felony child abuse by today's standards. I would have been removed from the home. But, in those days, it was just "strict discipline," or so I thought. Now, of course, I know better.

The effect of that circumstance was that I internalized a landscape where I believed I was an absolute failure. I was not good enough and never would be.

In addition, handling your own problems and never talking to anyone was drilled in my brain until I simply believed that was how the world worked.

The outcome of that circumstance was from my early teens until my early 50s; I suffered MDD (Major Depressive Disorder.) I was never diagnosed or treated but staunchly believing in my own worthlessness was the catalyst for catastrophe.

I spent my entire adult life trying to prove that I was "good enough" to my mother. I lived with the total absence of any real feeling of my own. I didn't know who I was, didn't know what it was like to feel anything for anyone, and did not trust myself.

Predictably, the consequences were three failed marriages, addictions, and chaos at every level. As I reflect back on this, the fact that I had a successful career path is nothing short of amazing. I was able to obtain and hold down high-level jobs for decades.

I made a lot of money and lived a crazy dual life of success in the corporate world with addictions, divorces, and disaster behind the scenes.

Something like you might see in a movie.

At the time of the accident described above, I was 51. I had already attempted suicide. I was divorced for the third time, and four of my ten kids lived with me.

Hitting The Wall

A few months later, that same son was severely burned in an accident where he and his friend were playing with gasoline. They told me later they were making Molotov cocktails.

Again, I was horrified, ashamed, and uncertain as to how to handle the burgeoning crises in my life. Still unwilling to reach out for help because I was afraid, I spiraled deeper into depression, misery, and lack of attention to everything around me.

In one final suicide attempt, I calculated the amount of cocaine required to kill someone of my body weight. I also calculated the amount of alcohol that would kill me from alcohol poisoning. I consumed enough of each of those to do the job.

For reasons I still do not understand, I did not die but spent the night in wild hallucinations face down on the floor of my study. After that, over the next few weeks, a series of events unfolded that constituted a divine intervention. That series of events saved my life, helped me get sober, and put me on a path to heal my heart block of worthlessness and create a life of meaning.

Wake Up Call

On a Friday in August 2007, a few weeks after my 2nd failed attempt to die, I sat at home getting ready to binge for the weekend. I was trying to decide where I would go to start the party. For some reason, I felt an irresistible urge to turn on the television before I left.

Because I made a lot of money, I prided myself and having all the latest electronics. I had a giant screen TV and all the sound system to go with it. The irony was I did not know how to turn it on because I wasn't much of a TV person. I just had one because "that's what you do when you make a lot of money."

My 16-year-old daughter obliged and showed me how to turn on the device. Because I never watch TV, I was unfamiliar with the programs offered. Somehow it ended up on a show titled Intervention. I had never heard of it. It is a reality show dealing with people whose families stage an "intervention" to get them to accept the help they need.

No one was staging anything for me, and I had never heard of this program. The protagonist for the show was a high-ranking executive with a cocaine problem.

I was astounded because I had never seen anything like it. I watched for about 10 minutes and turned it off in disgust. I would not watch this garbage, even though the sickness in my stomach told me I should.

After I turned off the set, I puttered around the house for 40 minutes or so. For some reason, I felt compelled to turn it back on. To my absolute amazement, that same show started from the beginning. We did not have a recording device. I checked the guide, and it was not scheduled.

I began to feel frightened and realized I must watch this.

The program played through, and the protagonist refused all the offered help. I didn't know what to make of what I had seen, so I decided to go to bed. It was approaching midnight. The program had upset me enough that I delayed my plans to get wasted and just went to bed.

Describing what happened to me during the night and the next day will strain all credibility. I can only report what happened.

I went to sleep immediately and found myself in hell. I could see and hear people, but I could not see their faces clearly. I was not in my body, and I have no idea where I was. All the events of the past several years were paraded before my eyes, including the betrayals, lies, illegal activities, recklessness, and stupidity.

I have never felt such emotional pain. The level of remorse and disgust I felt cannot be described in words. I cowered in a corner and felt helpless and hopeless as the scenes paraded before my eyes. I have never felt such abject pain, terror, and fear in all my existence. I cannot begin to describe the emotions.

After an unknown period of time, I heard a voice. It said simply, "It is enough."

Instantly, I returned to consciousness. I found myself in my bed at home. All the bedclothes were soaking wet as if a waterbed had burst. I did not have a waterbed. No amount of sweat or other bodily fluid could begin to account for the liquid that was present. I had no idea what had happened.

I looked around, and the sun was streaming in the window of my bedroom. That was impossible since my window faced west. I looked at the time and realized it was 5 o'clock the following afternoon. I had been absent for some 17 hours.

I was familiar with the wild hallucinations I experienced from my cocaine addiction. Daylight visions and paranoia had been a regular occurrence for me over the past few years. There was something completely different about this experience.

In addition, I was not using any substances before I went to bed. I chose not to because of the weird TV experience. I had no explanation for what happened.

I sat for an hour or so thinking about what happened and trying to figure out what to do. It was absolutely crystal clear that I had been invited in the most powerful way possible to instantly change my course of life.

I had no idea what I was supposed to do, but I knew that continuing the way I was going was not an option. I got up, showered, and dressed, and threw away $1000 worth of cocaine I had lying around.

From that event, I went cold turkey from $3000 a week to sober in one day.

We're Just Getting Started

I didn't know how to deal with life as a sober person. I knew I had to change everything about what I was doing, and I didn't know where to start. I had never spoken to or confided in anyone for 40 years.

I had no idea what was coming on the journey I was beginning.

It's one thing to suddenly become sober. It is quite another to face full-on the context, events, and circumstances that made you want to hide in the first place. I did not know how to act. I did not feel anything at all. The only thing I knew for sure was I was done with the drugs.

Divine providence works at its own pace. I went to work on Monday and did not know how to act. I pretended everythi8ng was normal. It was far weirder than doing the job under the influence.

In the position I held, I often received free tickets to games and concerts. They were usually very expensive and privileged seats. I guess people were trying to be impressive.

Tickets always seem to come in pairs, and I was single as I mentioned above. These tickets were to a Yo-Yo Ma concert at the premiere venue in Edmonton. Not wanting to waste a ticket, I ask in the groups I managed, "Who likes classical music?"

Joy, a woman in one of my groups, answered, "I do."

"Have I ever given you anything before?"

"No"

"Here you go, see you there."

The concert was astounding, and if you know Yo-Yo Ma's work, you know exactly what I mean.

Halfway through the concert, an otherworldly feeling I was now familiar with came over me. I felt as if a voice whispered in my ear, "You need to marry this woman."

Horrified and frightened, I immediately began arguing with the voice, citing my repeated relationship failures and the fact that I was in completely uncharted territory with my path forward.

The voice went silent, and the concert ended. The tickets were, of course, backstage passes. Backstage, the feeling came back more powerfully and added the caveat, "And, you need to tell her tonight."

Inside, I was having a meltdown with no idea how to respond. I argued in a futile attempt to avoid the direction I was receiving. I lost the argument.

I told her, and it went about like you would've expected. She thought I was crazy and wanted nothing to do with it. The divine always knows what's going on. Over the next two weeks, she had her own set of experiences that convinced her that this was her path forward.

Within two weeks, both of us had resigned our positions, made a commitment to each other, and moved forward into what would be the greatest adventure of our lives. As I write this, 14 ½ years later, the clarity and correctness of that divine instruction has been repeatedly manifest.

Moving into the Unknown

Neither one of us had any idea what the future would bring, but we both knew that divine direction had brought us together. Joy had heard all the rumors around the office about my addictions. I was forthright with her about everything that had happened, including the experience two weeks prior.

I made sure she understood exactly what she was getting into because I didn't want any surprises. I have never met anyone in my life so clear, so willing to trust the divine, and so fearless. She made her choice and never looked back.

You might think, "well, if I had such things in my life, it would be easy to change and eliminate my barriers." Let's be clear, the divine intervention that brought my sober transformation and the second divine intervention that brought Joy and I together were invitations. They were just the beginning.

Neither one of those events changed anything about the decades of depression which still had not been addressed. I did not tell Joy anything about that because I didn't know. I only knew the behavior that had come from that depression.

The process of getting help and overcoming the effects of lifelong depression was something we had to do together over the next several years.

I still did not know how to be in a relationship. Despite multiple marriages, I had never learned to have a friend or to trust anyone with my inner feelings. God was the only one who knew at that time Joy was the only person on earth who could make that happen.

The first few years were a complex and sometimes frightening journey as I began to learn who I really was. I had no idea what I was going to do for work. While I was now sober, neither Joy nor I had any idea how powerful the life-long depression would be in shaping how I dealt with our new life and reality.

We had to create a business or two. We had to figure out where we were going to live. I had ten kids whom Joy would come to know and who would need to figure out who she would be in their lives.

Some of the kids reacted very badly. Some did better. The old depression refrains in my head, "you're not good enough for this; you should fix it all; it's all your fault anyway," played loudly every time anything went wrong.

I didn't go back to drugs, but I had to develop other coping mechanisms and gradually change myself into a new person. For the first time in my life, I began seeing a counselor and talking about my history and the patterns of my life.

I had to discover what made me tick before and what I needed to do differently to have a life that was beautiful, purposeful, and what was intended when God intervened in the first place.

The main difference this time was that I was determined no matter what, I would move forward in a positive direction. I chose for the first time in my life to throw away all the old stories about who I was and stopped trying to place blame on anyone, including myself, for everything that happened.

I accepted responsibility for my own behavior and went on a journey of both making amends and forgiving everyone I thought had offended me. I had a long list of people that needed attention.

Some of that went well, and some of it went poorly. Those familiar with a 12-step addiction recovery process know about the step on making amends. Sometimes that goes well, and sometimes it is painful and difficult.

Some things brought struggle in our relationship. Rather than damaging our relationship, we made the conscious choice to allow each experience to be one of growth. We made solemn vows to each other, which we repeated often that no matter what happened, each experience would teach us and transform us into better people.

Creating a relationship is hard work and, at the same time, a work of art. In my case, three relationships were being created at the same time.

First, I created a relationship with God. It was clear He was involved in every step of my life, even when I was blissfully or stupidly unaware. He had patiently waited and guided until it was time for some dramatic action. Nurturing that relationship was the first key.

Second, I needed to develop a relationship with myself. Because I had always pretended to be whatever I needed to be in every circumstance, I didn't even know who I was. I began recording music. I reopened the recording studio. I helped Joy in her eBay businesses.

Finally, I chose to move into the coaching business. I realized my consulting experience doing difficult projects, combined with the dramatic transformation of my personal life, made coaching a beautiful opportunity. I realized above all; I treasured the experience of helping others overcome heart blocks and change their lives.

Third, I needed to develop a relationship with a woman. That beautiful angel who came into my life as the miraculous gift from a loving God. The one who had the courage to accept a staggering challenge. I learned to have a friend. I learn to trust another with my feelings. I learned to identify and articulate things that before were always under the surface.

Literally, in the space of two months, both of us quit our jobs, left the industry we had been in, created a new life, and started new businesses. We created a relationship and fought with unwavering determination to make it work no matter what.

We realized divine help, and divine power is available to everyone, and we learned to take shameless advantage of that help at every turn. We then learned to offer that love and help to others in every opportunity and circumstance that presented itself.

Trusting the Process

I have written the details of my journey in other books. This is simply a summary of the steps, however incredible, that took place to move me from broken to whole, from hopeless to powerful, and from completely depressed to on fire with energy.

One of the most important things I learned along the way is to trust the process. There is a God, and you are his child. You have been created for success and not failure. Every piece of help and power, and love you need to succeed in your life is available in the here and now.

I didn't always know that, and I stumbled around in the dark for decades because I did not look and would not receive. Receiving is a tricky business. My learning was that I couldn't just sit and wait.

Decisive action, continuous risk, and moving forward boldly was required at every step. There were plenty of stumbles and brick walls. But making the irrevocable choice to take responsibility for my life and do whatever I had to do to make it better was necessary to access divine help that was available.

The interventions in my life were just invitations. At any point and at every point, I could have refused the invitation, claimed it was too hard, and sat down to give up. As a coach, I often see this take place. People say it's too hard or they don't know what to do, or they have no choice.

My gift to you is an absolute assurance that you are not helpless or hopeless. If you learn to trust the divine process and claim your right to choose better in every decision, there is no limit to what you can achieve or how you can grow.

The Joy is the Journey

An old habit I had was to choose to live forever in anticipation of something not yet manifest. Some call it the "I'll be happy when…" syndrome.

God, as the designer of our mortal experience, intended the process to stretch us, cause us to grow and at times perplex and even temporarily defeat us.

I finally learned I could choose to be frustrated with that design element, or I can choose to lean into every circumstance in my journey. I have chosen now to be open to everything that comes and to consciously seek the development and encouragement available from every experience, no matter how hard.

The joy of life is not the destination. The joy is the journey. The sites and signs along the way, the temporary or long-term setbacks and challenges that have to be accepted, managed, and eventually overcome. How I deal with all this says everything about who I am.

I lived a lot of my life unhappy, waiting for things to happen or trying to make them happen. I expected to have joy and reward from myself or accolades from others when I got to the "golden ring."

The truth is far more elegant and powerful. Every day you draw breath, you can live the ultimate life. The ultimate life is a life of purpose, prosperity, and joy created by serving with your divine gifts. It has nothing to do with status, money, external accolades, or any of the other nonsense we worship.

Your joy can begin today. Hopefully, you won't wait until your mid-50s as I did, before I realized I had control. I am the supreme architect of my life. I am the master of my own feelings and choices. I do not control the weather or other external circumstances, but I am the absolute ruler of my own attitudes, actions, and feelings.

The wisdom of the creator and the design of the experience become more evident with each passing day. The joy of this world and this life truly is the journey.

Where can you go if you start today?

You may be wondering what all this means for you. You may be wondering how you could start right now, even if you believe everything in my journey.

I do not know your history, and I do not know the divine gifts you have been given. I do know you have infinite potential, and no one can limit you except you. I know you were given gifts and talents before you came here, and you had a mission and purpose you agreed to and were excited about. If you want to start today, here are some thoughts about how to do that right this minute.

First, listen to your language. How do you speak to others and especially yourself? Are you using the language of victimhood or the language of creation? Are you using the language of compassion? Choose to take ownership and speak in terms of your own worth and power to create your world.

Second, partner with the divine. Meditating or having prayer with a long list of demands is pointless. If you accept your creator loves you and planned this experience for your growth and development. Then acknowledge that and study out in your mind the best steps to take. Then in your supplications, ask for guidance and help.

Third, no matter what setbacks and problems occur, choose to accept those as normal parts of the process. Always ask yourself, "What is the gift here?"

In choosing that approach, I have learned so much and been blessed in more ways than I can count. There is always purpose and blessing to receive.

Fourth, make an irrevocable choice to be the divine creation you were intended to be. You may not know right now what this involves. You may not understand the struggles that lie ahead. Trust the process, have faith in the divine, and move forward boldly.

Remember this: Regardless of what has come before, it is never too late to matter and have a big impact as you choose to live your divine purpose.

KELLAN FLUCKIGER

Coming from a 30-year history of executive experience in the energy industry, Kellan held C-level positions in the US and Canada.

Extensive consulting experience in energy de-regulation and other high-pressure areas prepared him for the coaching career that he now enjoys.

The author of 13 books, with numerous bestsellers, Kellan now coaches an international clientele in business, inner work, and high-performance.

A life-long love of music saw Kellan start to write, perform and publish original music. He's owned a recording studio for over 40 years and is active in performing his music. He's also with a recording group that has charted #1 on Billboard and has performed in sold out concert halls across the United States.

Kellan also had a 40-year battle with undiagnosed and untreated Major Depressive Disorder (MDD), which led through a roller coaster of high-flying success and secret stints in rehab for addictions and a few attempts at suicide.

He now finds great joy in helping those who want to end addiction to mediocrity and realize their full divine potential.

In 2018, Kellan had a near-death experience as he lay in a coma for nearly three weeks while doctors scrambled to both save his life and diagnose the lethal strain of necrotizing MRSA, which had severely infected both lungs.

From that experience came several books, most notable is Meeting God at the Door - Conversations, Choices, and Commitments of a Near-Death Experience and his latest, Down from the Gallows.

Connect with Kellan at coachkellanfluckiger@gmail.com or his website at www.kellanfluckiger.com.

CHAPTER 11

Your Past Does Not Define Who You Will Become

Lakisha James

It was the year 1990. I just graduated from primary school. I was on my way to high school, and I was so excited. I was excited I was able to march in my high school marching band. I was able to be amongst new people and make new friends. I did not know what would await me starting the summer of 1990.

So, here I am. Preparing to enter the 8th grade. I grew up in a single parent household. My father was in my life but not like I would have liked him to be. I was anxious to start summer marching band practice. I would not say I was shy but, I was more of a girl that kept to yourself and was observant. Anticipating the start of this new experience was very thrilling.

Summer band practice started. I was a part of the clarinet section. I met some upper classmen and some people that would be in the same grade as me when school started. The marching band was a big family. I tell you though, I was not used to marching and playing a musical instrument at the same. It was exciting to say the least.

School started and I was embracing being a new girl at a new school. I've heard horrible things about first days in high school. I was a sub freshman and like everything else in my life, I enjoyed it. I already had my classes and knew where all my classes were. I started making new friends and gaining this newfound confidence. I was moving up and there was no turning back now.

One day at marching band practice I met this guy. He was a sophomore. He would come and watch us practice often. I think it was probably about one or two weeks before he approached me. He introduced himself and I reciprocated. We exchanged numbers and we started talking daily. Soon after the long talks on the phone and late-night talks, we started dating.

Now, I was in high school. I had boyfriends before while in primary school, but this was my first real relationship. You know when you're in primary school, you really don't date. You talk on the phone, flirt, and hope your parents allow you to go to the mall with your friend or with your sibling. At that point, you would be able to meet up with a boy without your parents knowing it. Did I just say that?

Things started to get serious with my boyfriend. Everyone knew I was his girl. He made that known. Every night we would spend long hours on the phone. We would fall asleep talking and sometimes we would listen to each other breathe. But it was okay. We enjoyed it. He would walk me to my classes and after school he would watch me practice with the marching band.

One night, my mother was working, and he came over. My sister, my brother and I were the only ones at home. My boyfriend and I went into my bedroom. That night, I lost my virginity. I was 13 years old. Not once, I remembered my mother telling me to wait until I was older or married. Not once did my mother say if you start having sex use protection...or better yet before you do, let's talk about it.

After I had given myself to the one person, I felt I loved, things started to change. We would skip school and get caught. One day, we were walking down the street hugging each other and his mother's vehicle approached us. She was angry and told him he would be in trouble once he got home. I would sneak out of the house to be with him. I did this for a while before I got caught. I ended up on punishment and was very upset at my mom. But why was I? I was the one that was being defiant. I was the one who knew I was not supposed to sneak out of the house in the middle of the night.

I would accompany him over his friend's house all the time. We would go to school for a few classes and then skip the remainder of the day. My mother never found out about the skipping. Not sure why, though. Good thing she didn't. After school ended, I would go back on campus and attend whatever extracurricular activity I was in at that time.

One night I was over his house. He had a room downstairs. Downstairs was like an apartment. There was a restroom, a bedroom, and a living room. We were talking and suddenly, he struck me. Not just once but several times. He was punching me for a few minutes. I could not contain myself. I was trying to protect myself and my face. Once he completed his rage, it stopped. I was crying profusely. He looked at me and he apologized. I went into the bathroom and my face was bloody and puffy. My lip was busted, and my eyes were bruised. I didn't look like myself. Not to mention, it was a school night. I had school in the morning.

His mother came to the top of the stairs and asked, "what was going on"? She said, what did you do to her"? He replied, "she's okay". I said nothing as my body and mind was still in shock. After his mom left, he hugged me and kept apologizing. I was looking like, what the heck just happened? I just got beaten. I had to go home and lie to my mom about what happened to my face.

We see situations like this on television. A woman's boyfriend or husband constantly abuses her, and she continues to lie about what is going on. Instead of building up the courage to leave him, she stays and hopes she can change him. It only gets worst. Hopefully, she does not lose her life before she is able to get out.

He took me home and the next morning, my mom woke me up for school. I walked into my mom's room and looked at her. She asked me what happened. I told her I fell and hit the corner of a table. She believed it. I missed 3 days from school to recover. My face did not look like I hit any corner of anything but my boyfriend's fist. That was a head on collision.

This was the first of several dating violence experience I had to endure. There were times we were at school, and he would see a guy talking to me. He would punch the guy and pull me and would tell me to come with him. Another incident I was at lunch, and I was talking to one of my male classmates. My boyfriend came from somewhere in the cafeteria up to the table I was sitting at and slapped my face hard in front of everyone and then he left. I was so embarrassed. I got up from the table and walked out of the cafeteria and started crying. I didn't tell anyone what was going on. I was too afraid. No one came after me because they were afraid of him.

Another incident we were at school. I was in class and someone from the office came to pull me out of class. I was told my boyfriend got into an altercation with another guy about me. I couldn't believe what I was hearing. He was so jealous and possessive. At the time, I didn't think too much of it. After time continued, he would tell me if I left him, he would kill me. So, you know what I did? I stayed. I stayed with my abuser for 4 years. Some days were good. Some days were bad. I never told anyone I was being abused. It became the norm for me. This type of abuse, well any type of abuse is not normal.

This is the year of 1993. My boyfriend left for the military. He went into the Air Force. He would call. We would talk. He was in Virginia. This happened for about a year before he was dishonorably discharged. He came back home, and we continued where we left off. The abuse and everything. You may be wondering why I stayed? I thought I loved him. He was my first.

One last incident happened when I was at work during the summer of 1994. I was a lifeguard during the summer. This particular summer, he came up to the pool I was working at. I saw him come through and I left the office where myself and other lifeguards were. We started to talk, and he struck me. He struck me several times. I didn't know what I did to deserve it. I couldn't believe he would come up to my job and do this.

I was crying. He left and I went back into the office. My Manager asked what was wrong with me and I told him, my boyfriend just struck me. He walked out of the office to comfort my boyfriend, but he had left the premises. Again, I was so embarrassed. This was the fourth and final year. I said enough is enough.

I had to take back control of my life. Even though I was young, I had lost myself. I had allowed this person to invade my life and made me feel I deserved this. I did not deserve this. No one does. It was something my boyfriend has seen or been abused himself and he thought it was normal for him to treat others that way.

After we broke up, I had no contact with him. I had to start my healing process. Remember, I had given this guy a part of me that I had never given a guy before. Yes, I was hurt, angry, and naive. I was manipulated into staying in an unhealthy relationship. I let me self be free from him. Free from bondage. Free from entanglement. Free from physical abuse. I didn't think about it. I focused on swimming, band, school and getting my youth back.

Years later he apologized. I accepted. There was not anything I needed to be upset about. It was a phase in my life where I was in an abusive situation. I learnt from it and now I can share my story to the next one that is experiencing abuse in any form.

I can tell you this, the dating violence I endured impacted my future relationships. I told myself I would never be in a situation or relationship I could not control. I had no control in that relationship. I allowed myself to not love, to only think of me. Thinking like that only hurt the ones that entered my life. This continued for years. It was LaKisha's way or no way.

I had a heart block. I didn't allow anyone into my heart unless I wanted them there. No one was there for years. Not until recently, I opened my heart and allowed myself to feel, be vulnerable and to be the woman God created me to be. My heart is open to love again. My heart is open to notice when someone is being genuine and want to be a part of my life and not harm me. I'm no longer the controlling woman that destroyed past relationships.

Overcoming Heart Blocks...

Step 1. Recognizing the trauma, you endured is the first step. Be able to call it what it is. You must love yourself enough to want more. You must want to be better. If not for yourself than for your loved ones. No one deserve to go on that dark journey with you.

Step 2. Affirm your life. Once you do, you will be able to speak life into any situation that comes your way.

Step 3. Give yourself time to heal. Healing is a process. It does not happen overnight. Stay strong and know you were created for greatness and life does happen.

Step 4. Be the voice for the voiceless.

Step 5. We don't have control over other people actions. We are only able to control ourselves and that is on Mary had a little lamb.

I am now a mother of two girls. I know God allow things for reasons. I now know why I experienced dating violence. I have such a calling on my life. When a person has a calling on their life, they endure. It does not feel good at the time but as times progresses it gets better. Once you are settled into the new journey, you will experience something else. But no means, do not allow yourself to be weary. You are a superior being.

Love yourself…

Be yourself…

Know your worth…

Pray…

Believe…

Do it Again…

LAKISHA JAMES

LaKisha James is the CEO and Founder of Designer Events by LaKisha located in GA. Their specialty is international corporate event planning, event design and set design for films, and plays. She holds a degree in Interior Design and Management with a concentration in Small Business & Entrepreneurship.

One of her favorite personal quotes is, "Every space is unique, and you make it your own".

Ms. James is the recipient of the 2019 "CEO on the Rise" award for Who's Who of Urban CEO's.

She was nominated for the 2020 "Talented CEO" award. Ms. James is the Atlanta Chapter Leader for the global women empowerment organization, World Women Conference & Awards (WWCA).

She also serves as Ambassador for Black Women Networking (BWN). Ms. James has co-authored 2 books. Her first book titled, Wake Up Winning No Matter What Because Losing is Not an Option Vol. 2 launched in January. Her second book was a multi-author international book project titled, "I AM: Releasing the Shame of Narcissistic Abuse and Transforming Financial Poverty to Wealth Beyond Numbers" launched in April. The book established Ms. James as an international bestselling author. She is Editor for Real Women Atlanta Magazine. She was nominated for the 2021 Leadership & Philanthropy awards for World Women V.I.S.I.O.N. Awards. She is the recipient of the 2021 Leadership award. She was inducted into the Marquis Who's Who in America for 2021- 2022. She is featured in the 2021-2022 Marquis Who's Who of Professional Women publication.

She is the Host of Talks with LaKisha with JSL Network, on the ROKU platform and I AM the Network. Talks with LaKisha are in pre-production. Her first show will air in September. She is the former Executive Director for Times of Expression & Refreshing Ministries (TER Ministries), a nonprofit based out of California. She is currently the Set Designer and Production Assistant for Saving Nina. The film is in pre-production.

Ms. James is also an Interior Designer, Mentor, and Speaker. She is featured in the first and second volumes of Who's Who of Urban CEO's magazine, EventPlanner.com, VoyageATL magazine, Shoutout Atlanta, Real Women Atlanta Magazine, Wall Street Select, EINPressWire, and 24-7 Press Release. As well as an Entrepreneur, LaKisha is also a mother of two, and lives by the statements, "Without God, I am nothing!" and "He has equipped me with everything I need to be successful!"

Email: ljames@mydesignerevents.com

Website: www.mydesignerevents.com

Instagram: www.instagram.com/designereventsbylakisha

Facebook: www.facebook.com/lakisha.rakestraw

Facebook: www.facebook.com/designereventsbylakisha

Twitter: www.twitter.com/designandplan4you

CHAPTER 12

Rising From the Ashes

Julie "Juju" Christopher

If you are stumbling into these next few words, it is not by accident. My intention is to share with you my direct experiences in hope to inspire you on your higher path.

My first heart block was when my dad left. To this day I still don't know the real reason for it. I was only 9 years old at the time. I continued to blame myself which fostered unhealthy behaviors and a deep-rooted craving for approval from others.

At the age of 15 I was victim of sexual assault. I was not allowed to speak about it because the aggressor was a close family member. I took a chance and told my mother about it. She said:" It's your fault, you shouldn't dress like this!" Feeling abandoned and unworthy, I wanted to disappear. Eventually I developed eating disorders like bulimia and was anorexic. I felt lost. I WANTED TO DIE and tried to exit this world with several suicide attempts. I didn't want to feel pain anymore. I felt powerless.

Although you might think this is the reason why I am writing this, this was only a speed bump on a very long and rocky road to Self-Realization.

We lived in a little house on the prairie in the South of France. From the outside, it looked peaceful and beautiful, like a masterpiece of

Monet.

When I came home that day, my guitar and a box with my belongings were left outside by the front gate. I knew this was a pivotal point in my life.

In a moment of weakness and in fear of winding up alone, my mother chose to marry a man that gave her an ultimatum "It's me or the kids!" I left that day and never returned. I was only 17, wounded and hopeless.

Shortly after, I moved to Paris and was introduced to the music industry where I worked as a music recording artist. I have tried my best to bury the Psychological Traumas that left me with upsetting memories and anxiety. I remember feeling numb at times, disconnected from myself. Music and creativity was my way to cope with pain.

I felt extremely vulnerable in this ruthless, male-dominated environment. Have you seen the movie 'Taken' with Liam Neeson? I was blind folded, raped, tortured, drugged, brainwashed and was nearly turned into a sex slave. Luckily, I have found a way to escape this horror.

When we learn self sabotaging behaviors, it is very likely that we start matching very similar scenarios unless we practice self awareness. It is critical at this point to seek help! The lasting effect of my childhood memories resulted in very poor self esteem.

Words of wisdom:

I had to first be honest with myself, take accountability and ask for help. With a heightened sense of intuition, I began to listen to my heart. Meditation was the key to my healing- A practice that can lead to spiritual breakthroughs. Traumas disrupt our body's natural alignment. It freezes us in a state of hyperarousal and fear. With the practice of Yoga my body image slowly restored. My nervous system repaired and I could finally tap into Self-love, forgiveness, acceptance. As a music artist, I am able to channel my pain into songs and immerse myself in the creative process. Volunteering also gave me a sense of purpose.

Practice this exercise daily:

Seat outside with your arms stretched out to the side. Visualize an ocean of peace at the heart center. Feel the expansion of your consciousness as you receive unconditional love.

In closing:

You are not defined by your past. God gave you the innate abilities to fight for yourself and the courage to step into your light. Ultimately, we realized that our heart blocks are universal gifts on the path to enlightenment .

" Surviving the experience is the healing" Juju

JULIE "JUJU" CHRISTOPHER

Julie Christopher, aka Juju, is the creator and CEO of Biztuition. Juju is a professional 'Enter-Trainer'- Music Artist, Speaker, Healer, Bestselling Author- She is a world-renowned expert on business intuition and host of 'The Mystical Entrepreneur' podcast.

It was her inner voice that led her to America with only $50 and a guitar. In spite of arriving as a homeless illegal immigrant who couldn't speak English, she had faith in herself to overcome the odds and manifest success.

Today Juju is widely recognized for her unique contributions to the business world. She has been interviewed on national TV shows like Dr. Drew, Nancy Grace, Legal View with Ashleigh Banfield, and more. Juju has also been featured as one of the world's preeminent experts on sites like Forbes and Authority Magazine.

Juju is also a VIP contributor for Entrepreneur, Thrive Global, and other media outlets, and has even graced the set of the popular television show Shark Tank!

Throughout her career, Juju has successfully helped entrepreneurs from all walks of life to navigate and overcome life and business challenges. With her keen power of Biztuition, she foresaw that a quantum shift was inevitable, and she quickly realized the need for leaders to seek help with modern-day difficulties like The Infobesity Epidemic.

Today, Juju leads her 'Mystical Entrepreneur's global tribe on the path to Self-Realization. You can find her at events and retreats...or chanting under a tree…

She is available for interviews & Live performances both for music and keynote speaking.

Website: www.Biztuition.com
Instagram: Juju_mysticalentrepreneur
https://www.facebook.com/julie.christopher.100/
https://www.linkedin.com/in/juliechristopher/

CHAPTER 13

From Resilient Mind to Resilient Heart

Beata Seweryn Reid

"Owning our story can be hard but not nearly as difficult as spending our lives running from it. Only when we are brave enough to explore the darkness will we discover the infinite power of our light."
- Brene Brown

Have you ever felt like there is some kind of a hidden force within you that is holding you back from achieving more, connecting more and living more? What makes you stay quiet when you want to use your voice? What keeps you paralyzed when your heart longs for change? What is blocking your heart's desires? We all experience many so-called "reasons" that hold us back such as fear, self-doubt, rejection, judgment, assumptions, beliefs, and even culture. But where do these blocks, often negative and disempowering, come from?

When you look at me today, you would never know what challenges I went through and how those dark moments transformed me. I had to "die" in order to give birth to the person that I am today. Twice in my life I felt as though I had died - once physically and once emotionally. And sometimes, when you are in a dark place in your life, you tend to think you have been buried, but in reality you just have been planted.

I was born behind the iron curtain in a small village in southern Poland, the youngest of four, wanting more out of life than what communism was offering. I was seven years old when I was in a car accident and suffered a serious brain injury. Due to the extent of my physical injuries, the doctor's prognosis was very limited in terms of my potential to live a normal life.

I was young and there I was answering one of the biggest questions in life: Will I be a victim of my circumstances or will I be a victor of my destiny? God did not let me die for a reason and I loved life too much to be a victim. But our childhood shapes our future self, and hearing from those I was supposed to respect and believe that I would be less than others created in my heart a very deep block of feeling inadequate. That became my darkest shadow for many years.

I moved forward. Life was good. Putting aside the limits that the doctors had placed on me, I worked hard to achieve my goals. Great job, amazing friends and I even got a bonus prize. I was in a relationship with this beautiful man. He made me feel important, pretty and special. I began to think that I knew what my life was going to be. John Lenon once said, "Life is what happens when you're busy making other plans." That couldn't have been more true for me. Just before our 11th anniversary, my beautiful man walked away. On that day I lost myself. The feelings of being seven years old again, rejected, helpless and fearful about the future came flooding back. Perhaps the doctors were right. I was not normal. And I was not enough. I reached what felt like my emotional death.

Rejection is a messy thing. It makes you believe less of yourself. When we are confronted by rejection, we are immediately faced with painful feelings of inadequacy. Depending on what and how the rejection is delivered, it can even break us in ways we never thought possible. Rejection destabilizes our fundamental need for safety, security, love, and belonging. It certainly did for me.

When healing from a traumatic experience, we tend to build invisible walls of protection that are supposed to protect us from potential danger of being hurt again. In reality, the walls keep us imprisoned from all the good that is awaiting out there for us. And I discovered that I was extremely talented at building walls. Shutting out the world became second nature to me. I had chosen my own emotional life of being miserable.

With time, I began my journey of healing and personal development and began to realize that what matters most is how we respond to what we experience in life. It's not what happened to us, but our response to what happens to us and the story we tend to believe that either hurts us or propels us forward.

We all have our own unique operating system - our thinking. This includes our beliefs, the way we process information, respond to life events, make decisions, see the world, and judge ourselves and others. Similar to a computer, in our mind we will continue to run certain programs unless we consciously make changes. But if you are anything like me, I'm sure you have found that reprogramming a computer seems a lot easier than reprogramming your own mind!

Why is it so challenging to shift our thoughts, feelings and behaviors, even when we can recognize them and know they need to change?

Well it's because we tend to deal with the effects (behavior, action, results) and not with the cause (when and under what circumstances the block was developed.) A lot of our beliefs, like in my case, were created in our childhood. So often, the stories become so ingrained, they almost feel like the truth of who we are.

Life is unpredictable and every new chapter will require a new version of you. That's why transformation is not an overnight process. It takes our consistent attention, effort and patience to update our mind to match the truth of who we are today.

Now, you might wonder: Can we change anything and everything about our life?

From my experience, no. Here is why. There are things that we have power over and there are so many things in life that happen out of our control. The challenge is to be able to distinguish between the aspects of yourself you can change, and those of which you have to let go. It reminds me of the serenity prayer: "God grant me the serenity to accept the things I cannot change, the courage to change the things I can, and the wisdom to know the difference."

Through all of my ups and downs on my journey to inner liberation, I learned that the only way to protect my heart against any adversity and recover in a healthy way is by removing the walls and developing a resilient mindset. What do I mean by resilient mindset? It is a mental attitude that sets a personal response and interpretation of situations. Resilience is more about how we choose to think about the circumstances we face! Too often in the past I was reacting with negative, victim-like stories of the events instead of responding with a peaceful heart. Today I know that the ending of my relationship broke me open and fractured so many of the walls and protective mechanisms around my heart that I didn't even know I had. It opened me to the things that needed to be healed. Only through full acceptance of the pain of the breakup was I able to meet the parts of myself that were screaming for love and attention. I really needed to meet those wounded parts of myself so I could create closure and start from there; moving forward in power, more whole, more complete and more aware. Awareness gave me distance from all the dramatic stories that were going on in my mind. You cannot grow yourself if you do not know yourself. And from that space I could start living life forward more deeply.

Although we cannot undo the past, we can heal from it and create a desired future.

Three steps to heal your heart blocks and to develop a resilient mindset.

The first step is CLARITY- Clarity defines reality and requires you to ask yourself tough questions. How did I get here? Where am I going? Why is it the way it is? What is my part in it? What's keeping me away from happiness? Identify what works well and what needs to be improved. I tried many tools in searching for clarity on my transformational journey, but the most powerful one turned out to be journal writing. Journaling is the fastest way to gain clarity. All you need is a pen and paper or your laptop and then just write. Journaling is a powerful tool that I use often for myself and for my clients to get out of my head and to open my heart.

To help you with clarifying your heart blocks, I invite you to do one of my favorite written exercises. Grab a pen and a paper and write the following questions: 1. What do I really, really want? As you noticed I used the word really twice. There is a reason. The first really usually is full of other people's desires for you and I want these desires to be truly yours and yours only. Please take your time and search your heart.

Then you are ready to move to the next question. 2. Why don't I have it by now? Write down all the reasons you can come up with. In the answers to the second question you will discover your limiting stories that keep you stuck and are the results of your life experiences. Your inner work starts here.

Step two is CONFIDENCE. Every time I was going through a challenging season in my life, I somehow doubted my self-confidence. I even judged myself for feeling that way. After all, I was always told that I was born confident. And then one day I realized that there is a huge misconception about self-confidence. There is no such a thing as being born confident. If so, as children we would not long for the environmental approval. Confidence has a lot to do with your self-image and what you believe to be true about yourself and the world around you. Remember that we always have two images, the one we see in the mirror and the one we hold in our mind. The good news is that since self-image is just an opinion, it can be changed anytime we choose. Why not start today? Funny how many great realizations come from life crises. I discovered what the entire world already knew: that confidence is a skill that comes with practice. The more you practice the more you believe in yourself and that you are able to figure things out. Confidence is all about expanding your comfort zone. Stretch it. One day at a time. Start with your thinking. Get to know yourself. The more knowledge and understanding you have about yourself, the greater will be your confidence. Remember it all starts with a thought. What you think you become.

The third step is COURAGE, in this case the courage to act. It took me a while but I learned that courage is not about waiting for better times to come but refusing things the way they are and going for something better. Nothing changes without your participation. And you must have a strong desire and the willingness to act. It's time to stop being afraid. Step out of fear and step into your power. As has been said, courage is not the absence of fear, it is acting in spite of having fear.

The courage you need is already in you. It always has been. It's often challenging for me to let go of how I imagined my life would be or who I thought I should be. When I chose to let go of these limiting expectations, I discovered that my ability for growth and my courage is immeasurable. Often the areas where we feel the most resistant to change-are the areas that we most need to evolve. For this reason, be aware of those feelings of resistance when they arise. These are your opportunities to stretch your comfort zone and exercise your courage.

Along this journey, as you would be with a loved one, be patient with yourself while you learn, grow, and figure things out. It is okay to change your mind about what you thought is your forever and redefine what this new chapter of life means to you. It is okay to raise the bar on how you treat yourself and how you believe you should be treated. Not knowing what you want or what direction to go is okay too. Think and act with an open heart for yourself and for others. Have the clarity, confidence and courage to allow the heart blocks to fall away.

BEATA SEWERYN REID

Beata Seweryn-Reid is an in-demand Life & Leadership Coach for Entrepreneurs, an International Speaker and a Change Maker.

Awarded as a "Woman of Excellence 2019" by the Women's Economic Forum in India, Beata has been a featured guest on a variety of TV, podcasts, summits, and workshops in the genre of self-improvement and well-being. Beata has been a featured speaker on Les Brown's "Power Voice Summit" and is the host of her own weekly live show, "Meaningful Conversations with Beata" where she interviews change-makers to raise awareness and inspire transformation. She is the founder of Beata Life Coaching, a unique platform of coaching to success through journaling. She empowers people and businesses to navigate through many of life's challenges such as job loss and business struggles by teaching them about the power of their own thinking and guiding them to adjust their mindset for better outcomes. She focuses their thinking on their strengths and their ability to meet challenges successfully.

Emigrating from Poland in 2011, Beata struggled with accepting her accent while adjusting to a new culture and trying so hard to blend into new surroundings. During these challenging times she realized that more than anything else, our thinking has the ability to either get in our way or to propel us to great success, whether personally or professionally. Today, Beata enjoys helping high achievers and entrepreneurs conquer significant changes in their own lives and ultimately seeing them break through their limiting thoughts, improve their leadership mindset, and achieve the life they desire.

www.beatalifecoaching.com

CHAPTER 14

Healing My Broken Heart

Lauri Schoenfeld

The sky is rumbling today in Utah as the thunder shakes the ground and the rain is weeping. It can be jarring when unexpected, and we often hide and shelter away from the storm. But, today I'm also reminded that rumbling can help us to gain awareness to a fresh and new beginning.

I had a rumbling a few years ago that shook me to the core. I was at the lowest point in my life, ready to end it all. I'd been in multiple spaces of abuse in my life, and after years of trying to be what everyone else wanted me to be, I was miserable. I still felt numb. Nothing seemed to work. I thought that I was getting nowhere, and even after my efforts, I didn't like what I saw in the mirror. My heart was broken so badly that I could no longer feel it. It was all just static. I sat with myself that morning, making a plan of how to end it until I heard laughing on the other side of the wall.

My children.

I paused and winced.

This felt like this was the only option, but I couldn't do to them what I saw my mother attempt many times. It forever left a mark of fear and worry of the day I would come home, and she might have succeeded this time—gone forever.

The rumbling came after the pause for me. Deep within my bones something ignited that I hadn't tried everything. My deepest heartbreak wasn't from anyone else who'd hurt me. It was how I'd hurt myself for years, over and over again. Every time I tried to be someone I wasn't for someone else because I didn't value me. Every time I said "no" to myself with my dreams and goals, and I called myself nasty names. Every time I showed up doing unhealthy things to numb the pain. It was all the times I blamed someone else or made an excuse for something I chose to do.

It was every time I didn't allow myself to speak my truth.

I broke my heart, and I betrayed myself. I didn't want to see that. It's easier not to see and pretend, but as I sat and wept there in truth, I knew. I could choose a different path.

I was at a crossroads of going back to what I knew in comfort or embarking on this new journey of uncertainty. I didn't know who I was or what that looked like. There were snippets and flashpoints, but most of my life had been checking in to see how others liked me first, and I responded to that. In this new space, it was like restarting all over. Hope and fear lived there.

What if I didn't like what I found out?

I knew that might be true, but this was something I hadn't tried, and that was much better than where I had been.

The first step that I took was to write a letter apologizing for how I've hurt myself over the years and asking for forgiveness to try again. Each day, I began writing down how I physically, mentally, and emotionally felt. This became my investigator journal, taking account of my journey on what appeared to work and what wasn't. I wrote down things I would like to try and things that I would like to do. Each week, I tried something new, and I did something I liked to do. I took some time away to learn how to listen to my voice and practice holding compassion for everything that would came up in silence. Often, anger and negative voices were what I heard. I would place my hand on my heart and say, "That's okay. I love you. I'm sorry I didn't listen to your needs. I'm here now."

I wrote down things that I'd like my kids to learn and started doing them for myself. You can't teach what you don't feel or aren't doing.

Each week, I did one scary thing to stretch me out of my comfort zone instead of saying no or making an excuse of why I can't.

Over a few months, I started feeling again, and the static lifted. As I sat with myself in honesty and love, the more my heart pieced back together. When I glanced into the mirror, I began to smile.

Every day is a journey of healing and checking in, as life will constantly give us rumbling. We're never done learning or getting our heartbroken, but we can fall in love with ourselves again each day. With the changing of the wind, we can get back up and try once more. What's waiting on the other side could be a space we've never explored before. It could turn out even better than we had imagined.

LAURI SCHOENFELD

Lauri Schoenfeld currently resides in Utah with her hubby, three kids, and dog Jack Wyatt Wolverine. She's a child abuse advocate, a Nancy Drew enthusiast, and is part cyborg. Teaching creative writing classes to her community is one of her favorite things to do. When she's not having long conversations with her characters and creating stories, she's hosting the Enlightenment Show, reading, or solving a mystery.

Lauri's a well sought-after speaker and a frequent guest with multiple writing groups, podcasts, and businesses, talking about Connecting to Your Artist, Embracing Your Fears to Succeed, and Learning to Love Yourself After Abuse.

She's the owner of Inner Enlightenment, a business built around connecting to your inner light and child within through stillness, creativity, play, and self-expression. Lauri teaches and holds creativity workshops, retreats, and one-on-one coaching.

LITTLE OWL is her debut novel coming out on August 31st, 2021. Visit her at www.laurischoenfeld.com

CHAPTER 15

Finding Peace Within

Manny Blue

In my personal experience there are many things that we can experience that can cause a heart block, whether it is a bad break up, a traumatic event, etc. A heart block can be detrimental to our way of life if we do not overcome it. It can cause you to miss out from opportunities and life changing events and from reaching that next level of life that you are looking to achieve or would like to achieve. Overcoming a heart block may take some time, but I want you to know that it is possible regardless of what caused it.

I am going to share with you two of my personal experiences, one of them I have only discussed with a hand full of people. I chose to chat about this specific heart block because I realize how it affected me, affected those around me and I didn't even know it at the time. One of the biggest mistakes I made growing up, whenever someone did something that wasn't nice to me or tried to do me wrong, I would retaliate by holding a grudge (a form of heart block) or wanting to do them wrong as well. I don't think people realize the amount of energy and time a grudge can take not just in your mind but in your heart or how it can affect your life. At first, I didn't know what triggered me to feel or act that way. Years later as I stepped outside the box to analyze myself and it is when I realized why I acted the way I did. My way of being, it was somehow connected from the events that took place when I was just a kid.

For a long time, I despised my father and held a grudge. I was two years old when my parents divorced. After the divorce, my mom moved to Puerto Rico and my father, technically became a ghost. He was absent from my life; he didn't bother being a father. Years later, he claimed that my mother took me away from him and that he couldn't get a hold of me and that infuriated me for many reasons. Why? Well, I guess he forgot that when I was around 7-8 years old, I told my mother that I wanted to meet my father. She had no problem doing so, but she warned me and explain to me why they got divorce. Apparently, he had a drinking problem, and he would become abusive whenever he drank alcohol. I guess she didn't want me to be disappointed. At the time I lived in Puerto Rico, therefore my mom booked the flight and back to New York we went. We all met at my grandmother's apartment. He was a friend of the family before my mom and him got together. Long story short, we took a walk, and I remember seeing this gold Batman toy, I asked if he could buy it for me, he stated that he couldn't because he had no money. Most kids wouldn't understand that, most kids would probably wine or catch a tantrum, but I didn't. We went back to my grandmother's apartment. Some time passed and more family members showed up, they decided to head to the supermarket to get a few things and cook a nice dinner. In that process my father pulls out a few bills out of his wallet to have them buy beer. Several boxes later, that he kept paying for, it is no surprise that he got intoxicate. The biggest part that hurt me, was that he lied to me. Claimed he had no money to buy a $10 toy but had money to buy beer and get drunk. I would have rather been told, no, I don't want to spend money on toys.

For some time, I hated him, despised him. I wanted nothing to do with him. Not because he didn't buy me the gold Batman, but because

I just could not figure out how can a parent not want to be in their kid's life and or lie to them. If his accusations were true regarding my mother "taking me away", why didn't he fight for me? It is what any loving parent would do. Did it made me feel unwanted? of course. For a long time, I had an empty feeling in my heart that I wanted to fill so bad. Some of my friends who had both parents in their lives, when they would go out together or go out of family trips, I was reminded of the missing piece that I didn't have. And that hate towards my father would creep up again. At times, jealousy would creep up because I wish I had my father in my life. Being a mixed Hispanic kid, it got so bad that I hated talking about him or letting people know that I was part Mexican because of him. I just simply wanted nothing to do him. Because of that situation, I made a promise to myself when I was just a kid, that whenever I became a dad, that I would never be like him. If things didn't work out with my kid's mother, that I will do everything in my power to be in their lives and that I will fight to the death of me. My mom later dated and remarried but I couldn't find it in my heart to accept another man in my life. This heart block caused me to become rude and ignorant towards my mother's new relationship. I feel bad thinking about it now because I was truly a brat. I was thinking about myself and not my mother. When I was around 18 years old, I was at my grandmother's place and my father happened to call, she said "hold on Manny is here, you can talk to him". At the time I didn't know who was on the line, I thought it was my mom, she just said here take the phone. I took the phone and I said "Hello!", the person replied with, "It's your father", immediately I went into angry mode, I replied "my father? I don't have a father, you're not my father. Funny how now you want to talk after all this time". He proceeded to tell me that he had no way of reaching me or finding me. I quickly ended the call. Well, long story short, in 2010 he came looking for me. Want to know how he found me? He used my social security number to find me. My first question was, I thought you had no way of reaching me or finding me? Why didn't you want to be in my life then? Why now?

How could I accept a man that claims to be a father and wants to be in my life now? Did he expect me to welcome him with open arms? That train was long and gone. I was a grown man and at the time a father of 2. I felt angry and still had hate in my heart towards him. It wasn't until a few years ago that things change. I realize this heart block was affecting me, the people around me and the way of life that I wanted to live and provide for my family. How can I live a harmonious life, full of love when I was still carrying hate and anger in my heart? How can I be the best that that I can be and set a good example for my kids if I was still from time to time speaking negatively about my father? I was in the audience at a networking event and I remember hearing one of the speakers talking about a father and son relationship, and in the speech he said, "you must forgive him, you have to find it in your heart to do so". I felt it was directly to me. I knew that it was what I had to do if I wanted to get to that level of peace in my life. I decided to let it go, accept what happened and start fresh. When I did, I felt such a weight lift of my shoulder and in my heart. After speaking with him a few times, I made it clear that we may not be able to have the relationship that he and I wished that we could have but, that he is more than welcome to be a grandfather to my kids if he wanted to and we shall see what happens as times goes by. I realized after speaking with him several times that he was still living in the past and that he was a bit immature for a grown man. I came to the realization that there was nothing that I could do or say to change him or the way he thinks. I had this experience with other people in my life. I had to learn how to deal with it without affecting my peace, because I want to live a peaceful and harmonious life and I am sure that you do as well. Holding a grudge took a lot of space in my heart and caused me to retaliate with individuals that had nothing to do with the issue. For example, when

I was 16 years old I fell in love with this girl who broke my heart. You may ask what does a 16 year old know about love. I tell you, I never felt for another girl like that again. Everything was great and from one day to another it all ended. I couldn't figure out what happened, if it was something that I did or didn't do. Till this day I still don't have the answers. It caused me to have trust issues with my future relationships. Because of it I hurt a lot of people emotionally, I became her and broke hearts. They didn't deserve that, but it was the aftermath or my personal experience. I wanted answers that I was never going to get. It made me angry, confuse and because of that other people that didn't deserve to get hurt, did even though they were not part of the problem. We don't mean to do so but it definitely can happen. There were seeds that were planted, and it slowly grew but not in a positive way. I had to find a way to chop that tree down and plant new seeds.

With everything that I experienced in my life, I quickly realized, the first step was acceptance. Accepting what had happened. Truth is, there are things that it is completely out of our control. My advice to you is, focus on what you can control. Trying to get in control of something that you can't, it is going to cause you aggravation and headaches. Realizing that it was out of my control I chose to focus on what I could control. This can take time and may not be the easiest thing to do. But it is what I personally had to do. I accepted what happened. Next, take a step back, step outside the box and analyzed your situation. Asked yourself, how did I get here? How did I allow myself to get here or feel this way? We cannot change what already happened but, what could you do differently next time around? If I can give you some advice, do not dwell so much on the signs that you missed or how you could have done something differently, because you will drive yourself crazy, it is already done and unfortunately, we cannot turn back time. But learn from the experience.

Let's touch base on the following steps that personally helped me in every situation that I have had to deal with in life that caused a heart block for me at different stages of my life and I am sure that they can help you as well.

Acceptance: Not easy in most cases. As I mention before, somethings are out of our control. Some people simply just wont change. Just because we accept someone for who or what they are, it doesn't mean you have to force yourself to be around that individual or situation. For example, with my father, I had to accept that he chose not to be in my life and made-up excuses. I had to accept that he is an immature grown man that still lives in the past. I wish that I could help change him way of thinking, but I can't. Although I accepted what happen and his way of being, it doesn't mean that I have to deal with it. I forgave him and found peace. If we talk, I know what to expect, therefore I keep the conversation short.

Forgiveness: The hardest steps. It was important for me to forgive. I realized that carrying such weight on my heart, hate and unanswered questions wasn't doing me any good. I realized it was affecting my way of life and would affect those around me at some point in some shape or form.

Focus on what You can control. The minute I realized that I was wasting my time on the things that I couldn't control, helped me put my focus on what I can control. Whether that was my way of thinking, the way I reacted to situations such as rude people, etc. I hold myself accountable. I remind myself that it can and will get better because I am in control.

Seek help or resources and be vocal. Don't be afraid or ashamed about what you are feeling, thinking, or going through. It will not only help you but also help someone that may be experiencing a similar situation. You can save someone's life and not even know it. There is absolutely nothing wrong with asking for help or speaking to someone such as a therapist. We all should have someone that we can speak to.

Each of us will face different situations at some point in our lives that will lead to a heart block. Some much more complicated than others. I want you to know that you got this, you can overcome it and remember that you are in control. I believe in you. Follow the steps and you will find peace within and the weight on your shoulders and heart will be no more.

MANNY BLUE

Manny Blue, an entrepreneur, author, and philanthropist. Who previously entertained his audience on the stage as a performer/recording artist, has traded in his blue spiked hair and dance moves, for a suit and a laptop. Blue finds himself encouraging and motivating his audience to chase their dreams, live their best life via motivation but also change their relationship with money and become financial literate. Manny Blue is the founder and CEO of Blue Legacy Capital whose mission is to serve the underserved communities when it comes to financial education!

CHAPTER 16

Turning Heart Blocks into Hope

Pamela Aubrey

"Our heart blocks need not be a life sentence and they can serve to become the building blocks for the foundation of our greatest successes."

Many babies come into this world celebrated, wanted, and loved by two parents who have planned and dreamed of bringing a child into the world. Some do not. When they don't, it can set the stage for all manner of personal challenges, and an ongoing endeavor to overcome what can come from that one differentiator.

My birth mother became pregnant with me at age 20, in the worst of circumstances, in many ways. She was separated from her then husband, who was violently abusive. She was living in the basement of a man's home from her church, essentially homeless, with almost no resources.

Having already been married and divorced once before, my half sister being just a little more than 2 years old and the man who was my birth father wanting us to just "go away", she had little recourse. At one point she discovered that someone had cut the brakes in her car after an accident that she was fortunate enough to survive. After having the car looked at to determine what had gone wrong, she realized how fortunate she was, but also how dangerous her situation was.

Not one to be easily deterred, my birth mother carried me to full term anyway, sending many letters to a Christian adoption agency to determine how she might proceed with surrendering me for adoption. Ultimately, she kept me for 21 days, and then she surrendered me as planned, and I was legally adopted. The loss of our relationship was the birth of my first heart block, one that would impact the entire course of my life.

As many adoptions were at that time, in 1975, mine was closed. I was not to learn who my birth mother was, or the full extent of my story, until I met her in 2008.

What I remember most about that time in my life was the feeling that there were so many things that I wanted to know but didn't have the heart to ask her about. There were so many mixed emotions, and while I honored her decision to surrender me, I felt I couldn't tell her about the pain that had existed throughout my life because of it.

The years between my birth mother's decision and the realization of it's significance were littered with moments of trauma and pain and there was no room for grieving. If anything, adoption was made out to be the solution to the problem of a "sinful" mother who didn't deserve to have a child. I didn't understand the judgement of her, even at a young age, but I remember feeling like somehow I too was "tainted" because of her behavior.

Meeting her also brought me face to face with the pain I had lived in, even as a child. Some days it was physical, some days just emotional. I accepted it as normal, and went on with life, never speaking a word of what I felt inside.

It wasn't until I became a teenager that the pain inside seemed to bubble up so intensely at times I thought I could no longer bear it. At one point I planned to end my life, just to stop the pain. When the time came that I felt I should do so, I wasn't at all afraid, and rather, I felt a sudden sense of empowerment, like I finally had a choice in my life that only I could make. But in the stillness of the moment a voice whispered to me that it wasn't my time to go yet. I chose not to go through with what I had planned, but I still had much navigating to do to come to a point of breakthrough.

While I was raised in a minister's home, the environment was such that I learned early I would have to take care of myself, fly under the radar, stay involved away from home and keep my personal issues private. This is how I operated throughout my teenage and young adult years. I was independent, focused and motivated as well as a successful student and leader.

I eventually married and had my son, and it wasn't until I had a minor head injury 5 years later, and I couldn't take care of myself like I had to that point, that my life started to unravel. Suddenly I was in a position of barely being able to get out of bed and perform the most basic daily functions. My ex had long since stopped taking an interest in my well being, and we separated. I knew at that point in my life I had to start asking for help.This was a huge turning point for me because up until then, I had relied on myself to get where I needed to go. After several weeks of struggling and finally going to stay with extended family and see doctors, I began to regain my footing and I was able to resume a somewhat normal life. My memories wouldn't return fully for years, but I was able to operate day to day, enough to survive.

As the years went on, the fallout from emotional, mental and legal attacks against me from our eventual divorce began to severely impact my son. I fought to gain ground for him in the midst of toxic relationships, no support systems, and financial struggles but I rarely felt I was.

Then my birth mom passed. She had been one of my closest confidantes, and supporters, during those dark times. I didn't find out until after she had gone and I was devastated that I didn't have a chance to tell her goodbye.

I buried my emotions in work and meaningless entertainment, not sure how to move forward or deal with what had happened and not being able to afford therapy.

After filing and losing a custody case, my ex left my son and moved to HI with his new wife and her son. His abandonment came as a relief and a heartbreak as I watched my son get blamed for his father's departure, while simultaneously breaking free from his influence and behaviors. I had felt helpless to stop the pain he was creating in his life and even he expressed relief at no longer being forced to spend time with him. Still, I knew the damage was done and it became my mission to do everything I could to help my son get past what was happening. I had no idea where to start though, and he was tired of trying therapy. As the months turned into years, I wondered if I would ever find the answers we needed, and yet simultaneously that I couldn't ever give up. I was determined to keep fighting for him, not ever realizing I needed help just as much as he did, and how pivotal my own healing would be to his.

I eventually started attending free support groups at a local church, uncovering the dangerous patterns I had learned to live in and finding new ways to approach situations. I sought out healing through local Reiki groups, and found I was being drawn into the world of energy work I had briefly encountered as a massage therapist several years before.

This was a major turning point, and after almost 10 years of struggle and living in survival mode, I found myself beginning to experience hope again. I realized that I didn't have to take the journey alone, that others had and were in similar, and even worse situations. Yet, somehow, just by being able to share our stories, I was finding healing.

I also began to understand the complexity of my trauma and what it had created in my life. I began to realize I had unconsciously chosen people who would abandon or abuse me. That truth alone was pivotal because I realized that was something I could change. I also knew there was more work left to do, and I spent many months learning how to change old patterns and see them for what they were.

For over 3 years I continued learning and searching, and eventually found EFT. Short for Emotional Freedom Technique, this odd technique took me entirely by surprise. When I first started using it, I found it hard to believe this "tapping" idea could actually amount to anything. However, as the months went on, I began to experience significant shifts in my overall health and mental state. I also began to see opportunities I hadn't before, and after a few months, I found myself easily moving away from toxic people and situations. I noticed I was finding more success in my work, and I began planning a move that would allow me further freedom and closer proximity to my family. As the years progressed, I dove into the study of energy psychology and began to fill my "arsenal" with weapons for any battle.

Within just a year's time, I made the cross country move, started an EFT certification training course, and doubled my income. I was making huge strides in my personal and professional life, simply by consistently focusing on the goals I had set out to accomplish and using the tools I had gained in the previous few years to achieve them.

The pain I had felt so much of my life was finally beginning to dissipate and I was gaining massive momentum in the pursuit of my dreams. Since then, I have interviewed some of the most successful personalities of our time, now work with some of the most influential people on the planet, and my network is composed of hundreds of highly successful and heart driven human beings.

I also work with the world's top mindset coaches and have helped facilitate the realization of emotional, spiritual and mental freedom in the lives of thousands. I now live in a world of financial, relational, spiritual and emotional abundance.

And, to me, what is most extraordinary is that what has happened in my life can happen in anyone's life. I now know that with the right guidance and support, anyone can heal, and they can begin to move toward healing by taking these few key steps:

Accepting we don't have to face our pain alone. It's important to show ourselves compassion by being open to receiving help and explore the resources available to us that can help us navigate difficult waters, without the added pain of feeling alone.

Determining what we really want and committing to pursuing it wholeheartedly, despite any challenges or opposition. We need to consider deeply what we want to happen going forward. If we want to stay in our pain for a time, we are entitled to do so and should know that we deserve to make that decision for ourselves. At the same time, if healing is our final destination, we need to take the steps necessary to get there.

Keeping an open mind and being willing to explore new ways of healing. When we face our traumas, we need the opportunity to experience a wide range of feelings and thoughts, and allow ourselves to explore those. Sometimes that means we might look to new kinds of treatment or therapies that can help us cope with them. In my case, that ended up to be a mixture of things, and that can look different for every person. Part of the journey is listening to our hearts and seeking out wise voices to help guide us.

Remembering what we've already overcome. Think about the times you've struggled before. You made it through those days, and you probably came out the other side with new insights about life. This time may be different, maybe far more difficult even, but you have what it takes to get through it.

Finding small things to be grateful for. Sometimes we lose sight of all that IS going right when something difficult happens. For this reason, we need to be purposeful about being grateful, even if it's for something as small as a blooming flower or our favorite ice cream. From the smallest bit of gratitude comes the ability to shift our focus and change our state. While this can be a temporary change, we can support it with journaling, positive music, meditation, prayer or any number of healing modalities, including Heart Math, that help us experience more positive emotions.

While we all face traumas of many kinds, even the current traumas we face as a collective, we all have the power to not only overcome them, but to transform them. Our heart blocks need not be a life sentence and they can serve to become the building blocks for the foundation of our greatest successes.

In truth, it is in those horrible moments, when we are faced with our deepest traumas, the ones that tear at our souls, twist our hearts like pretzels, and leave us wondering where God is and how these terrible things can happen, we are actually being shown the fullest extent of our greatness. And whether we can see it in that moment, or whether we choose to wait, avoid it and allow ourselves moments of suffering, grief, and even turmoil, we can always come back to the truth of who we are. The truth that we are creator beings, that the decision to move forward, let ourselves be revealed, and release the things which are holding us back from doing so, lies solely with us. When we claim that truth, we can remember who we really are. Remember that we, alone, have the power to choose our own expansion and freedom, and when we choose it, we step into the world of miracles.

We must also remember that choosing to claim our power is neither right nor wrong, just two different paths, with different outcomes and different experiences to come with them. And, that each, in time, can lead us to another moment of decision where we can choose differently if we so desire; that the path to joy, hope, redemption and freedom always lies within our reach. It is this power to choose that has propelled us forward as a species for millenia and allowed us to overcome the worst of circumstances, personally and collectively.

When we begin to truly understand this, we will realize we are capable of accessing and utilizing the power of the Divine, which has been gifted to us all, and begin creating things far beyond what we have dreamed of. It is then that we know, with a deep conviction, mixed with wonderment and gratitude, that our heart blocks were really just stepping stones to an abundant and victorious life.

PAMELA AUBREY

Pamela Aubrey is the owner of Rising Innergy, a podcast host of two podcasts, Rainbows and Real Life and The PA System, a writer, business woman, Reiki Master, intuitive energy healing practitioner and visionary artist. In her career she has had the great pleasure of training and working with some of the world's top mindset coaches and their teams.

While her early life was filled with challenges, and she suffered a variety of assaults as an adult, these traumas became the basis for her greatest successes. On her journey of awakening, she discovered her own power through connecting with Divine Intelligence, and finding the tools that would change her life forever. She also discovered a love for energy work through EFT and Reiki, as well as her gift of receiving intuitive messages for others, the ability to interpret dreams, and the many ways she could help others shift their life forever with the use of some basic tools and principles.

Since then she has interviewed some of the world's top mindset experts, shared virtual stages with other experts in the coaching space and was given a set of writings, The Divine Life Journals, which she was led to share with the world.

Today she spends her time building her businesses, writing, painting, and advocating for others in her community and sphere of influence. Her passion continues to lie in her work as a trauma recovery facilitator, helping others create legacies of freedom, abundance and miracles.

Links:
www.risinginnergy.com
www.Pamelaaubrey.com
www.thepasystem.live
IG: @realpamelaaubrey
FB: https://www.facebook.com/pbaubrey/
Clubhouse: @realpamelaaubrey
Podcasts:
The PA System
Rainbows and Real Life
Books: (available on Amazon)
The Divine Life Journals
The Magic of Me Journal for Teens

CHAPTER 17

What if Letting Go Meant Rising Above

Erin Baer

When I look back at my life, the life I have lived there have been many trials, tribulations, and experiences which have been challenging. Then there have been good, great, and badass moments all which have changed my life in monumental and positive ways.

I have been raped, beaten, nearly killed, bullied, abandoned, abused and broken. I shouldn't have survived, but I did! Why? Having a difficult childhood, I never knew what the possibilities could be for me. Yet I hoped that they would be better than I could imagine. I just needed to start climbing my own mountain and creating my own path, my elephant path. That's exactly what I did until my mountain was moved by an earthquake, a period in my life that I never expected, plunging me into the darkness of abuse.

Looking back, I know when my biggest heart block happened, I just didn't know it when I was in the middle of the devastation that was known as my life. The tipping point of abuse and rape happened in my earlier adulthood. It forever changed me and how I began to look at myself and my life.

The following excerpt from the book: From Beaten to Badass, by Erin Baer describes the experience of rape and the devastation that results.

Rape is a horrible thing, a demoralizing, excruciatingly painful act. When it is happening, all you can do is numb yourself, praying it will stop. You can try to fight back and I did, I tried, but he pinned me to the bed with every ounce of force he could. My face pushed into the bed, my arms stretched out and pinned by each of his hands around my wrists and his disgusting body pressed against mine. He penetrated every ounce of my innocence. This monster, who I tried to convince myself cared for me, this monster who always apologized and promised he wouldn't hurt me, he deflated my over and over again until there was nothing of me left. I eventually got a hand free, found an object and threw it at him, hoping to make it stop. It stopped, but the damage had been done. I got away, but I couldn't escape. He grabbed me, he beat me, and I froze, covering my face and head. After the beating stopped, I stayed in the bedroom, crying myself to sleep. I had never felt so ashamed, dirty and scared.

Rape is painful; it's demeaning and it breaks your soul.

It shatters your existence into a million little pieces and you have no idea how to pick them up and glue them back together in hopes of making it look whole again. The scars of rape run deep, they are ugly and they burn. They never go away.

That abusive and toxic relationship I found myself in was one I thought I deserved. At the time, I didn't know I was the victim of abuse. I thought I was in a relationship with a mature, charming man. Afterall, I didn't have much confidence to begin with, and well, being in the relationship with a monster who was disguised as a "nice guy" I believed everything he said. I believed the words that came from the monster's lips each and every day. I assumed I should feel lucky that he put up with me. Due to my insecurities, I thought that I would never find anyone who could possibly love someone like me, a woman who was so damaged. I believed it, I believed all of it. How could I not?

This was someone I thought actually cared for me. So, his words must be true. I was alone, isolated, and I didn't have any friends or family that were really around to witness the shattering of my soul each and every day. I didn't speak to anyone about what was happening behind closed doors. I mean, would they believe me anyway? The monster was adored by his friends, co-workers and all who met him. He was not bad to look at, charming and charismatic. I mean, I fell for it, so why would anyone else be any different? I was an educated and successful woman; I couldn't possibly be a woman who would let another abuse me. Yet, here I was, taking it. I was a woman whose self-worth was so diminished that I would believe anything this monster said, because I did. He had me fooled. When I was in the "real" world, I would put on my happy face, while underneath it was a tortured soul who just wanted to be loved. I would tell a story, which was the biggest lie I had ever lived, but at the time I really thought I was living the life I wanted.

I didn't like what I saw when I looked into the mirror. Staring back at me with my own big brown eyes, was a woman I did not recognize. I was a woman who felt shame and had imprisoned myself in my own shattered heart. I realized when I looked deeper into my own eyes, I saw a woman whose heart and life had been broken into a million pieces, but that woman wanted to change that. I didn't know where to start. I had ended the abusive relationship, and most would say that I had nothing to show for it. However, they were wrong, I had a little ember inside of me that was waiting to be reignited once again. It just needed to be seen by me.

Going through an abusive relationship and rape changed me. The abuse wasn't the worst part. It was the rape. It deflated me, made me feel worthless, unlovable and lifeless. I have always been a believer in God, with faith in Him, in a way that I knew everything would work out. Yet I wasn't quite sure of that anymore. I know that after the abuse and rape, God wanted me to trust Him as I once did before and for me at this moment, that was hard. I was angry, I was mad, and I guarded myself so much so I began to build a wall that would be impenetrable. I didn't trust, I didn't trust people, especially men, I certainly didn't trust myself and I really didn't trust God.

As I was driving to work one day, the one thing that kept my days straight was listening to music on the radio. A song came on that changed me and the direction I decided to take my life. God works in great ways before we even realize He is there, before us, creating stepping stones for our own benefit. In the midst of my storm and the aftermath of abuse, I was doing everything I could to keep it together, to save face and to not let others know I was broken, truly broken.

The song that started to play was by Third Day, Cry Out to Jesus. In that moment God spoke to me and told me I was enough; I was going to be okay and just to take one step at a time. With His help I would see that this was all a part of His plan. I just needed to trust Him.

Being abused and raped shattered my trust and kept me on guard. I built a wall, stone by stone that no other person could penetrate. I realized that it was me I was keeping prisoner, rather than being free from the hell I had been through. A hell a monster created, but a prison I locked myself in.

It was in that moment as the song played, I cried, I cried out to Jesus, I cried and begged the little girl within to forgive me, and that I would never allow her to be hurt again. I began taking small steps. I began by telling myself the truth of what I have been through and how it wasn't my fault. It was a lot to take in, a lot to own and a lot to forgive. I wasn't very forgiving at first and I knew that I couldn't do it alone. I sought out therapy that was provided by the courts as I was not only broken, I was broke, so broke that I was in the red every month. Our judicial system is not perfect, yet for me when I needed parts of it to work, it did. I was able to seek both individual and group therapy and work through the traumas I had endured.

The hardest part of my journey was learning that my life was headed in this direction at no real fault of my own. The trust issues that arose, were a long time coming. Through therapy, you could say my eyes were opened and the blinders were removed. I thought that this abusive relationship with the monster I had just escaped from was the first for me. But as I worked on tearing down the wall of stones, I came to realize that the wall had been built throughout my life from all the traumas I had endured. It was this recent relationship that became the tipping point for the last stone to be placed, closing myself off from the world.

At 27 years old, I felt lost, defeated, as if nothing I had done before mattered. Who would love me, this mess of a woman? Afterall, I didn't recognize myself; I didn't like myself and I sure didn't love myself. However, I knew the only way to become who I wanted to be, was to give myself grace and love. It was hard, uncomfortable. Yet I was willing to try. As humans, we are given free will, the choice to make changes, and our emotions are a part of that. I got to a point that I wanted to get back to me, the person I was becoming before the monster snuffed me out like a flame of a candle in a hurricane. I already knew I couldn't go back to being who I was after everything I had gone through, yet I knew I could be stronger then ever before.

I couldn't move forward alone. I needed God. And to be honest I wanted Him to be a part of it. I found my faith, because honestly without the faith in God, I don't think I could have found the little bit of strength I did have, to get back up. I was scared! What if God really didn't love me, what if I had disappointed Him so much that He gave up on me? Those were lies, lies that crept in through the cracks from the words of the monster. The monster fed me so much hate and disgust that I thought it meant everyone, including that God felt that way. Yet, it wasn't.

Once I began opening up to my therapist, it allowed me to open up to my friends and mostly myself. I realized I didn't trust a single soul, but

I had to take the hands that were reaching out to me in faith. Having faith seemed a lot easier than having trust. Because to me, having faith meant I didn't have to feel as much. Having faith meant if it all crumbled, I could blame God. It meant I could distance myself from the responsibility of not feeling it all fully. I realized that this was not a one-day task, but rather a life-long journey that I was embarking on.

As I began the emotional and mental work, I felt the need to work on my outside appearance. I started working out because I thought if I looked good on the outside than everything would be good on the inside. I hired a coach and entered two bodybuilding competitions in the figure category. I was able to focus my energy into working out, eating clean and numbing myself and my emotions through the sweat, tears and sacrifice that came right along with my training. I thought I was on track to finding me. I was, but what I didn't know is I was about to take a real hard look in the mirror without warning -- a mirror that would truly reflect what I was hiding behind my wall that no one could climb and one I couldn't see through.

I competed in my first competition in October 2009, and then my second later that month. I did well in both shows, yet the second show was slightly different than the first. I was competing with teammates in the second show whereas in the first show, it was just about me. After the second competition, I broke down. Not only that, I started beating myself up inside for what I felt was a massive failure. I was in the dressing room in the basement of the venue where the competition was held. I thought I was just talking to myself, not just in my head, but out loud where two of the women who worked the show happened to be just feet away from me.

You see, my teammates took it all, they earned first place and overall, whereas I, in my classes, took 4th and 5th place respectfully but still felt like I had failed in my opinion, and thinking without justification that I disappointed my coach and teammates. With tears running down my face, I expressed to these ladies how much of a failure I was, that I wasn't good enough, I would never be good enough and the worst part was I actually believed it. Those ladies wouldn't have it. The first lady said, "Don't you dare, don't you dare speak about yourself that way!" The other, "You know what kind of guts it takes to do what you just did?"

These two ladies continued to speak to me in a way that allowed me to receive the message. The message of feeling proud of myself, my efforts and to not compare myself to others. That my only competition is myself! How could I possibly do that? Was I even worth my own competition, I thought to myself? Old habits die hard, and that was one habit that seemed to reign in my life, comparing myself to others. Yet in that moment, I knew they were telling me the truth and it was in that moment I found a little trust worth holding on to. The two ladies continued and spoke to me in a way that made sense. They told me again, I needed to be kinder to myself and proud of my efforts. To know why I was doing this. They embraced me and went on to explain that my reasons for competing needed to be for me and no one else.

I know what they were saying to me in that moment was all about the competition and how I was treating myself. Yet, their words rang true to me on such a deeper level. It was important to treat myself with kindness and to remember to do whatever I chose for me first. I was frightened because if I let go, I had to believe that trust was waiting to show me the way to my freedom. The other choice that came with trust was faith – faith in God, faith in my recovery, and faith in the next chapter of my life. Let's face it, at the end of the day it really isn't about anyone else when it comes to our own lives. I was exhausted of living for everyone else, I was at the end of my rope and all I needed to do, was let go. Letting go, meant letting go and falling into the unknown. I was frightened because if I let go, I had to trust and trust was just not something I had. I had faith though and that faith showed up. It was at that time that I also realized that until I could love, trust, and respect (LTR) myself, I would never be able to love, trust, and respect anyone else.

I had been in the dark for so long, that I was comfortable. I was afraid to let go as a positive affirmation of myself. Yet, just maybe, holding on was really anchoring me to the negative, critical me as being unworthy. This time letting go was really my only option. Though I was afraid to fall, I had to rethink and so I did. I finally let go in faith, blindly stepped forward into my darkness and this time I rose. I began to rise out of the darkness, and as I did, the one question I had for myself was, what would my life be like if it was full of light? I wanted so desperately to tear my wall down and have light within my world again. The faith I held onto allowed me to take steps, to let go and opened the door to the possibility of trusting again.

Each day my faith grew, which was directly tied to my trust. First, I had to trust God, that He loved me and He would never abandon me. Second, I had to trust my therapist and know that she could see what I couldn't see. That's where it started. Having trust in both her and hesitantly in God, it allowed me little by little to start trusting myself. With each stone I tore down, my trust in God, my therapist and myself began to grow. It showed me that I was the only one holding me back from the life I wanted to live; a life that I designed and one that I could feel good about.

Overcoming the heart block of trust wasn't an easy feat. I still have days where my trust is tested. But just like everything in our life, it takes time and we can only take one step at a time. Why is it that we feel the need to rush the process? For me, rushing steals the purpose from the journey and it's only ourselves we are doing an injustice to. So, dear reader, realize that building trust is a life-long process in which you can find self-love and acceptance with each step you take.

Since the abuse and rape, I have been on a journey to find and be authentically me, the badass (best person) I know I am and not be defined by my circumstances. My healing has taken a lot work, years of therapy with more to come. Talking it through, feeling all of it and being honest with myself I have been able to discover that I am my own HERO. Life is not a fairy tale, and it never will be. However, we, each of us, can be the hero in our own story. I decided to choose me for me. I also chose to walk with God daily, be with the people who love and believe in me, and to always approach life with a trusting spirit - even on the difficult days. This has led me to create my own elephant path. An elephant path is a path that you create, one that has never been walked, and one that will never be walked by another. The elephant path is unique to you, because you created it intentionally with every single step of your journey. My best advice is to live the life that you have designed, to create your elephant path and to be your own HERO within your story. After all you are the only one qualified to rescue yourself.

Through it all, I have developed a way to walk in my faith through all the seasons in my life. Becoming your own HERO takes work, takes time, and takes looking into your own eyes. You have to have love, trust, and respect (LTR) for yourself. You have to have faith in yourself and to know you are worth fighting for, for you - no one else. How does one truly become their own HERO? I have developed a way to always walk in faith that works for me. One, I know can work for others. Life isn't always going to be sunshine and rainbows. In fact, we don't get the rainbows without the storms. Becoming my own HERO was a process. Each letter of the word HERO stands for something. H stands for Heal, healing yourself is vital to move forward. E stands for Empower, from being able to heal, it allows you to Empower yourself which ultimately Empowers others. As we navigate through our journey, we find strength within, bringing us to the R, which helps us build Resilience to get through the times when we feel stuck in our storms. The O stands for keeping an Open Mind and Open Heart. Without an Open Mind and Open Heart, we close ourselves off, behind the wall that we built to contain the darkness. This is where the letting go of the darkness to search for the light begins. Now that I have seen my life with light in in it, I don't want to lose it. Keeping my mind and heart open allows me to trust. It doesn't mean that I don't struggle; it doesn't mean I don't have my doubts periodically, but holding onto the ember within shows me how to give myself love and grace. I believe it can do the same for you. Remember you are not defined by your circumstances, you are a Badass, you just have to get back up. Life is a series of breaks within but that is how the light gets in.

ERIN BAER

Erin Baer is a thriving entrepreneur and lives her passions as an Author, International Keynote Speaker and Empowerment Coach. Being a survivor of domestic violence and sexual assault, Erin began telling others her story of grace and grit on her road to recovery. This sharing of her personal story became the basis for her book, "From Beaten to Badass". The powerfully worded personal memoir gives readers the strength, hope, and courage to keep going and become the BADASS women they were always meant to be. Erin also founded the organization Beaten to Badass to empower and support those who have been beaten down by life. Her life's work is to enable beaten down and silenced women to once again be strong, courageous, and proud. Erin decided to be the positive voice to show beaten-down and silenced women that their circumstances don't define them, that they don't need to be beaten down in life, and that they too can be their own heroes. Through her coaching and speaking, Erin encourages you to look within yourself where you will find the power to unleash the badass in you. You may feel defeated and feel life is unfair by the cards you were dealt. However, the only way you lose is if you don't learn and you don't get back up. You are a badass!

Also, Erin is a Certified Life Service Center of America, LLC (LSCOA) Speaker

beatentobadass.com

CHAPTER 18

Healing is a Journey, Not a Destination

Karla Docter

I thought I was healed. I thought I was over this hump, done with all the healing and done with the trauma. I had a good ten-year break, or did I add to it by avoiding and repressing new things?

I had it all. I had a job that fulfilled me, and that I loved doing. I was making a difference. I was serving survivors of domestic and sexual violence, creating awareness of issues that were important to me, interviewed in the news, and trained law enforcement and professionals throughout the state. I was nominated for Woman of the Year, and recognized as a Woman Making A Difference, an Achiever Under 40, and as Oklahoma's 21 Leaders of the 21st century. I helped create the first sexual assault awareness 5k here in Oklahoma, improved programs, and even started teen sexual assault advocacy programing and services. I was the lead on writing grants, bringing in millions of dollars to our nonprofit agency to help provide critical lifesaving and healing services.

You see, prior to all this work I was doing, I had experienced a decade of domestic violence, sexual assault, raped, and robbed at gunpoint. This led me down a very dark and scary path. I had so much anxiety. I thought everyone is out to get me. I couldn't trust men. I couldn't trust friends, teachers, my school, strangers, bosses, or coworkers. Everyone was a threat to me. I felt like I had something that someone always wanted, whether it was my body, my mind, my spirit, my energy, my soul, my job, material items, my money, my support. I felt like I had been stripped down to nearly nothing after being robbed and held at gunpoint, it would take me sometimes, maybe three hours just to get in my home from my car.

I would be triggered by a cat, noise or a person as I was getting out of my vehicle. I would hear something or see something. I would be triggered so much that I would hop back in my car, lock the doors, and drive around the block and try again, and again, and again, and again. Sometimes it would take me hours to get into my house.

From the age of 15 until 25, I was in emotionally, physically, sexually abusive relationships. There were countless times where people violated my body, mind and soul. The relationships would always start off loving, sweet, supportive, and happy, but then a shift would happen, and I was suddenly called fat, dumb, ugly, and worthless. I was told that so much, that I started to believe it. They stalked me. They isolated me.

I was also sexually harassed from previous employers, coworkers, and customers for another decade, by working in the food and service industry, and an auto parts store. I was consistently reminded that my body was not mine and that I was dumb and worthless.

In college, I was raped by one of my best guy friends. After that happened, I reached out for help and told my best friend about it, and she said, "are you sure that happened?" So, I wrapped all this stuff up in a pretty bow and I tucked it away with walls, chains, duct tape, locks, and barbed wire. I thought if I can try to pretend like none of this ever happened and maybe it will just go away.

In my attempts to repress all the bad things that have happened in my life, I also repressed the good things too. I didn't know it at the time, but I started to lose control of my drinking. I was using it to cope from the trauma. My body kept score of all the wrongdoings that had happened to me. Drinking was an easy way to numb and forget about all the shame, guilt, filth, and rage inside of me.

It came to the point where I had no more fight left in me.

It took getting a DUI (driving under the influence) to start my healing journey. That DUI pretty much saved my life. I started learning about rape and domestic violence. I started to dive into self-healing and self-care. I was able to find comfort and validation for the experiences in my life. There are so many incredible books that helped me just like this book that you're reading right now that helped me feel seen, heard, and understood.

Journaling played a huge role in my healing journey and is still something that I do every day. The more I learned, the more I knew that I was supposed to help others who have also experienced things like me. I knew that I didn't go through all of that just to go through it.

After one and a half years of healing, I accepted a position to work at a domestic violence shelter to work at a shelter. I was on the right path, working with survivors, filled my cup. I was constantly affirmed that I was on the right path and doing what it was that I was supposed to do and I was really good at it.

About a year later, I moved to Oklahoma for an incredible job opportunity. The person I was dating at the time wanted to move to Oklahoma to go to law school. I told myself, "if I get this job, then I'll go". They hired me over the phone. I dedicated the next ten plus years of my life to helping others. I was positive, hopeful, helpful, and took initiative. I was called to do the media interviews. I was really making a difference for others and my community. I was also working long days, on call 24/7, and worked nights and weekends, but I always put on a positive face and was happy to serve.

At the time I thought I was really good at mentally punching in and out from work. But what I come to realize now, is that I didn't myself the space to feel and release my emotions. I created new heart blocks. I focused so much on pouring into others, my team clients, the community that I forgot to pour into myself, and I didn't address the root of the problem. I was losing myself in the process. I told myself that I needed to remain strong for the clients and my team. And although I mentally punched in and out of work, my heart didn't punched back in.

The Universe would give me opportunities to release these feelings and emotions, but I was trying so hard to do it right. I felt a lot of pressure. If I would get emotional, I was reminded that it's unprofessional to do that at work, so up went a few more walls and heart blocks.

Everything we did was so confidential that the only people that I would be able to talk about it with were coworkers, but I still felt all alone, especially when I moved up into management because I had to be so much more stronger for my team as my team grew. I had to be professional, and I didn't want my superiors to know that I couldn't handle it or that I was stressed. I was so blinded by all my walls and protections. I couldn't even hear my gut anymore. I didn't trust myself. I had felt like an imposter and couldn't trust my own judgements or making decisions. In the meantime, I started to lose my sparkle.

Then Universe/God/Divine Source Energy, whatever you call it, sent me a life raft to leave that stressful, but important job. I got pregnant and I was offered a position at another nonprofit that was an 8-5 job, with no on-call time, and no team to supervise. I thought I had an opportunity to get my life back I always joked and said that the only way that I would be able to leave this job was by death or pregnancy. So, I guess pregnancy, it is because there's still so much work for me to do. I was ready and excited to become a mom and start this next chapter. When I was three and a half months pregnant, I put in my two weeks notice.

The weekend after I gave notice at my passion job working with survivors, I discovered that my marriage might be coming to an end. My whole world came crumbling down once again.

As I was wrapping up and packing up a decade's worth of work and memories, I was terrified of what this next journey was going to be like that I was about to embark on. I started having panic attacks again, just like after I was robbed and held at gunpoint and all those other traumas, and now I'm pregnant. I carried all of this pain and fear to myself, and I cried, and I cried, and I cried, and I journaled, and I worked out and I took care of my body and my mind, I had the tools. I knew the tools.

I went back into self-development, learning and processing. I was meditating. I sought out counseling, but I still felt so alone and shameful and like a failure. I carried a ton of responsibility. Some of which was not mine to carry. There were only a few people that I could really talk to about what was going on, but still, they didn't know all the details. I felt like a fraud to the rest of the world, and I had to show up and pretend like nothing was happening. Up want some more walls, more heart blocks. It was excruciating hiding my pain inside, but I didn't know how to let go.

I was miserable, but once again, I just put on that mask of a happy face. I had a secret, and I was terrified about what the future held for me and my child. Am I going to be able to do this as a single mom? How am I going to be able to provide for my child? Am I going to lose my job? My security was gone, and the rug was pulled out from underneath me. I was in pain, and I was praying that all this fear and worry wasn't going to transfer onto my son or worse that I would be so stressed out that I would lose him too.

I felt like I was being robbed of all the joys that come from the miracle of growing a human. So once again, everything I knew had changed in the matter of a weekend. I can see now, that this pain was an opportunity for me to release my unfelt emotions and lower these walls. These heart blocks around my heart. And trust me, I cried. I released, I felt, but the heart blocks and those walls were so strong that even when I was in counseling and she would ask me, how does that make you feel?

I had to look at a picture of a feelings wheel because I had repressed all of my emotions, the bad and the good. Just like when I had experienced that decade of trauma, when I tried to forget that it all happened and I tried to repress all of those emotions, those memories, those feelings, my subconscious mind repressed it.

This began my next level of healing because after the birth of my son, I was fired from that life raft job. I knew that it was coming, my gut was telling me. As I was going through the healing process, I could hear my inner guidance, and I was starting to feel my feelings. I could listen to my gut and notice the signs. I was becoming more aware, and I knew what was coming. I had faith that this was just another sign that I needed to go all in on my business. The night before I was fired, and I saw a sign of a cross made by a shadow of a street and stop sign. I pulled into the parking lot and started crying. I looked up at the sky and said, "if me getting fired means that it's time for me to go all in on my business, I'll be okay." The lights started flashing on the side of the building and I felt the confirmation. I was on the right path. I knew that God/Universe was conspiring in my favor, and this gave me the space and the time to heal and to build my coaching and speaking business.

I continued to enroll in programs and courses to help me personally and professionally. All of those not only helped me, but they added additional tools for me to use for clients. I signed up for a manifestation program, and what I didn't know at the time, was how much I needed this program. When I signed up for this program, I was really hoping to work, manifesting real love and business and money and wealth and prosperity and health. I wanted the typical entrepreneur dream of time, money, and location freedom. I want to be with the love of my life. I want to feel love.

This is when I started going really deep into my healing journey. While, I have felt huge transformational shifts from books I read and other business trainings and coaching I invested in, but I had no idea how healing and transformational this program was going to be. As I went through this program and did the inner work, I started to find me again, who the Karla I was before all this stuff happened.

Honestly, the biggest gifts that this program gave me, was helping me get to the core of these heart blocks. I started on a journey of learning and about consciousness, the subconscious mind, universal laws and principles, energy work, shadow work, inner child healing and somatic healing therapies.

I started to strip back and peel back all the labels and belief systems that everybody else had placed on my mind, body, and soul. I stopped taking on everybody else's truth as my own. I started challenging them by doing the inner work and journaling, writing it out, and then speaking to my peer group about my discoveries gave me healing and peace.

One of the biggest, most life-changing things that I learned was that worthiness is my birthright. Worthiness is your birthright too. You don't have to do anything to earn it. Nobody can give it to you. You just have to claim it. And if you have a desire on your heart, it's meant for you. You are worthy of it because you are the person who has the desire, and God/Universe wouldn't place that on your heart if it wasn't meant for you. I had it so wrong before I thought that I needed to do something to be worthy of it, of receiving the love or the money or the things that I had to sacrifice all of myself, that I had to try and save the world.

I discovered a deeper meaning to forgiveness, and how by not forgiving and releasing is only hurting ourselves. Forgiveness does not mean that what others did was okay, it means that you are just no longer going to allow that other person or situation to hold power over you anymore. I love doing the energy work and cord cutting practices, as I know that they have helped me along my journey.

I then learned about Human Design (which is helpful for discovering who you are and what brings you fulfillment), energy clearing techniques, emotional freedom technique (EFT), rapid relief technique (RRT), hypnotherapy, inner child work, shadow work, Reiki, breathwork and so much more. Other techniques that I use are shaking, where you physically shake out and remove blocked and stuck energy, dancing, rage dancing, or anything that allows yourself to actually feel and release the feelings.

Every time that something triggers me, I know that there is a "Blesson" a Blessing and a Lesson in that moment that I can learn. I see my triggers as an opportunity to release a block to step into my next best version of me. The next time you are triggered, think about how it is making you feel. Take out a feelings wheel if you need to, just like I used to use. But give yourself the space to release that block now, because if you don't they just come back and the triggers get bigger and bigger, hence the last part of my story and the rug being pulled out from underneath me.

There are opportunities for us to release these stuck feelings, emotions and energy within our body. But we are often taught that it's not okay to feel the way that we feel, so we sugar coat it, paste some positivity on it, put on a smile and go about our day because we have to be strong for everybody else. Well, that's what I did for that next decade, and everything came crumbling down. So now I'm committed to doing the inner work. I can feel, process, and release new things more easily when I do it as they happen. That way I don't have to have another huge traumatic earth-shattering event, and if it does, then that's just another opportunity for me to release and to heal some more.

All these things took me to the next level of healing and removed those heart blocks. I no longer have to deny my true self or repress my feelings and emotions. In turn, I am attracting more of what it is that I want in this world and creating an even larger impact than I ever thought was possible.

While this chapter and part of my life is still unfolding and evolving, I can say that I have never felt more grateful, fulfilled, and joyful. I can't say what with certainty what the future holds for me, but I know it is going to be incredible because I get to co-create it. I do know that my life will include a lot more abundance, love, joy, and fulfillment.

So, to recap, here are some of the ways that I overcame my heart blocks and how I help others, journaling, mantras, and affirmations, meditation, breathwork, EFT, RRT, shadow work, forgiveness work, shaking, dancing, sound bath healing, human design, soul purpose astrology, inner child work, energy work, energy shifts, rage, dancing, dancing, spirituality, quantum physics, universal laws, working out, movement, yoga and grounding in nature to name a few. I created trust for myself, others and God/Universe to be able to receive my desires. Additionally, I invested time and money in coaches, mentors, healers, programs, practitioners, books, counselors, and peer group support systems.

I decided what I wanted and then worked on removing all the things, getting in my way, which started by me doing the inner work. I cleaned out my environment, physically, mentally, emotionally. I created winning routines. I ate healthy and treated my body with love and respect. I embodied my higher self, the next best version of me. I discovered and embraced that worthiness was my birthright.

I think that from a very young age, we were told and taught that it's not to be okay to be who it is that we are. We're always "too" something too fat, too skinny, too smart, too stupid, too emotional, too stiff, too crazy to this, to that. So, we repress these parts of ourselves.

Who are you? If you were to remove all the labels and roles that have been placed on you and think about what you want, like what you really want just for you, who are you?

The more that you heal and show up as the you, that you were created to be, the more beauty love and abundance will come flowing to you. More people become attracted to you because they can see how authentically you, you are. Every time I'm ready for the next level, it's like I go into training for it, and I peel back more layers to and heal. This is what will prepare me for the abundance, for the opportunity to serve more people, to reach larger audiences, that this is all part of the journey. Healing is a journey, not a destination. We will always be continuing to work on our healing journey.

And while the process is simple, it's not always easy. So, if you're reading this right now, please know that you are exactly where you're supposed to be. And now you have some tools and it's time that you can take some action.

The core to overcoming the heart blocks for me was to commit and decide that I was no longer going to avoid what I've been through and to allow myself to feel and release all the emotions, stories, and programming behind it, emotionally, physically, and spiritually. To invest time and money into my healing journey because I couldn't afford not to.

I didn't want to wait another day staying where I was, because I knew that there was something greater for me. Although I didn't a one hundred percent know what I wanted, but I sure knew that it was not this. I truly believe that the more that we try to suppress and avoid the longer we are postponing our joy and fulfillment, allowing ourselves to fully express our emotions, feelings, and beliefs, and to physically move out, stuck energy in our bodies is the key. Find yourself a journal and start to get all the things out of your head in a non-judgmental way, release all the shame behind the way you are feeling. When emotions come up, allow yourself to fully feel it, express them, give yourself that space and grace to process it.

Universe/God, Divine Source Energy is giving you triggers, which is an opportunity for you to process it all commit to healing, invest in a coach, mentor, healer, or someone you feel aligned with to help you through this process. Having this person with you will help see the blind spots that you cannot see. And they're going to stick with you because like I said, it's simple, but it's not easy. You might want to give up, but having someone to keep you accountable, who's there for your ultimate success is worth every penny. Remember, we are all strong alone, but together we are limitless.

So, in short:

1. You decide, you want more love, joy, fulfillment, and abundance, whatever it is, decide that you want it and know that you are worthy of it. Worthiness is your birthright. You don't have to do anything to earn it. And no one is more worthy than anybody else. If you have a desire on your heart or mind, it is meant for you otherwise you would not have it. Give yourself permission to remove any excuses and dream big. And you can start all of this here at www.venturelifecoaching.com/ideal.
2. Commit and declare to doing the work. The inner work block off time to commit to yourself. You may think that you don't have the time, but that is what you are telling yourself, prioritize you because no one else is going to do this work for you. And you can't give to others, which you can't give to yourself.
3. Invest in finding someone to support you on this journey. Someone who understands what it is that you've gone through and already has what it is that you want and desire. This can be a coach mentor program or someone who can be an unbiased guide on your journey. You can't afford not to do this. This person is going to help you do the inner work that you have committed to doing in step two. And this accountability is priceless.

4. Actually DO the work journal, meditate, find stillness in silence. Start to uncover and release all the things that you have been repressing and avoiding. Start building the know love and trust for yourself. The more you can process and release emotions, limiting beliefs, labels, the closer you will be to what it is that you desire. Most. I like to say I have a she-shed filled with tools to choose from. Some I mentioned some earlier, but it always starts with the basics with the journaling meditating, finding that silence. This is something you can start today for free.

   And if you want to go further, faster, heal faster, and find, then find that person that can be that support and guide for you along the way. You do not have to go through this alone. There are so many of us who specifically do what it is that we do to help people just like you, because we were there. And we know the importance of having that. And we want to give that back to you.

5. Remember that this is a journey, not a destination. The healing journey is a lifelong practice, but the more you do it, easier it gets, I am happy to support you on this journey. And I am sending you so much light love and healing, my friend, you got this. Remember, just start that, want to start with one thing that you've learned from this book and all these incredible stories and get started my friend, because you are worthy and deserving of that. And that is your birthright.

I love you.
To be continued...

KARLA DOCTER

Karla Docter is a Transformational Speaker, Author, Coach and Survivor. She is the Founder of EMPOWERCON, an international women's empowerment conference and retreat, and Venture Life, LLC. Karla is on a mission to empower, educate, energize and equip others with the skills, tools and resources to heal and transform their lives.

In addition to founding EMPOWERCON and Venture Life, LLC., Karla is a survivor of over a decade of domestic abuse and sexual violence, and then worked tirelessly as an advocate, mentor and trainer for survivors and professionals for over 12 years. Knowing there was more for her to do, she received an Elite Life Coach Certification and then began to transform lives through coaching, training and speaking to reach people around the globe in 2016.

Karla is a Co-Author in "The Brilliant Awakening 2.0, Awakening Narratives of Triumphant Overcoming Women". She hosts in-person and online events, workshops, masterminds, group coaching programs, EMPOWERCON, retreats, membership programs, and co-runs a local networking group.

Karla received her Bachelor Science in Criminal Justice, Minor Psychology and Certificate Forensic Science. She was also a Certified Domestic and Sexual Violence Response Professional, a graduated from the Oklahoma Victim Assistance Academy and many more certifications and trainings. Throughout her career, she has had the honor to be appointed to serve on the Sex Offender Management Team, Oklahoma Governor's Task Force on Sexual Assault Evidence Collection and the Human Trafficking Task Force, just to name a few.

Karla was named by the Journal Record 2017 as a "Woman Making a Difference", 2015 an "Achiever Under 40" and by the Business Times "21 Leaders for the 21st Century". Additionally, she has been recently featured in Edmond Business Magazine and several other blogs and events. In her "spare" time she volunteers and participates with several organizations including YWCA Oklahoma City, Edmond Women's Club, Oklahoma City Women's Networking Social and various other community events.

Karla is frequently called upon to provide both personal and professional development training and workshops. She has trained thousands on the issues of domestic violence and sexual assault throughout the state and has served on multiple committees to enhance community awareness and promote systemic changes for survivors. Additionally, she has been featured in the news dozens of times and has been seen in the community as an expert on the topics of domestic and sexual violence.

Since leaving her non-profit career working directly for survivors and serving her local community, she has been a full-time entrepreneur, transforming lives through coaching and speaking to reach people around the globe. She has been immersed in learning and teaching about the power of the mind, and how changing your thoughts and beliefs can transform lives. Additionally, she helps others learn how to they too can heal themselves and overcome life's traumas and obstacles.

Karla loves to help other women Know, LOVE and trust themselves, others and the Universe, so that they can Attract and Receive love, people and opportunities that set their soul on fire.

Karla would love to hear from you!

Connect with her on social media, and get your free Create Your Ideal Day Guide here:

https://www.facebook.com/karladocter
https://www.instagram.com/karladocter
https://linktr.ee/karladocter
https://joinclubhouse.com/@karladocter
https://www.linkedin.com/in/karladocter/
https://linktr.ee/venturelifecoaching
http://www.venturelifecoaching.com/ideal
https://www.venturelifecoaching.com/

CHAPTER 19

Diamond Heart

Eliza Conley- Lepene

What is a Heart Block?

Hawai'ian locals understand the importance of both love and healing. In Hawai'i, they approach everyone, and every living thing, with the Aloha spirit, which encompasses love, compassion, peace, healing, and light. This energy and spirit is the universal verbal and non-verbal communicative message of a brotherhood, and sisterhood of compassion and love, and the understanding that we are all connected. All Aloha energy sent out, is also the Aloha energy that is returned.

Aloha is not just used for hello, and goodbye, but used as a term that literally means, falling in love with, and love, is the way of life.

The locals of Hawai'i know what it is that is so enchanting about Hawai'i, that truly situates them in a place unlike anywhere else. They call it your "Aloha Moment", when you fall in love because realize it too. I find it may be difficult for some people to "arrive" at this moment, because we are stuck mostly in the mind, easily distracted by the lights, our phones, work, and daily stressors. Stressors sometimes have us hanging on and white knuckling the steering wheel of life, prevent us from Hanging Loose, and finding aloha for others, and within ourselves.

If you travel to Hawai'i, locals hope that you find the ability to hang loose, enjoy, and relax into life. It is hoped that you can immerse yourself in the healing energy and environment that will surround you. The trees, the water, the mountains, the flowers, the food, and most importantly, the people. It is desired that you are greeted, and left with aloha, that enchants your heart so much, that you yourself, will continue to share the Aloha Spirit with the rest of your world, once you return home.

This "heart block" you have been reading about is real and is described most explicitly through an energetic healing practice called Reiki. In Reiki, a "heart block", is explained as a block in what is known as the Heart Chakra. Reiki addresses the energetic fields of the body in 7 Chakras. The Heart Chakra is in line with the heart and is commonly known and represented in the color, green. The Heart Chakra is the fourth chakra, and it is the center of the 7 Chakras in relation to the energetic body.

Why is this heart block such a big deal? In Reiki, it is said that all energies pass through the Heart Chakra. The Heart Chakra serves as the filter for all energies, emotions, thoughts, and experiences. Any deficiencies within the Heart, can therefore affect the health of the body, mind, spirit, and relationships with others. Therefore, the Heart Chakra is chief in charge in how we relate to people, the dynamic of our relationships, and depending on its condition, is how we live life, how we love, and exhibit compassion.

Reiki healers are known for their ability to balance the Heart Chakra along with the rest of the energetic body. Their goal is to open closed, or restricted chakras, or slow hyperactivity in the chakra. This is done in all 7 chakras to balance the ever-flowing energy in the body. Reiki providers have been practicing this universal form of energy healing since 1914, and it is largely attested as a beneficial, and sacred energetic healing practice.

What Caused Your Heart Block?

I have lived a very lonely life, yet, I have loved very many people, beyond a measure that most people cannot comprehend, very little to none, have reciprocated. I have waded in the waters of the darkest hell not many could imagine. I believe I watched abuse objectively from a young age hoping to learn something, somewhere, and I have learned that it's easier to hate, oppress, and bully, than it is to love, and to help.

I began developing a "heart block" in my Heart Chakra at a very young age. I would explain this to look like a small kimberlite rock. With every traumatic experience, or bullying situation I was pulled in, the rock grew much larger. The more abuse I witnessed/endured, the quieter I became, and the more depressed I found myself. Yet, outwardly, I compensated for this by being extraordinary to others.

I spoke words of love, inspiration, and empowerment to others yet internalized every ounce of abuse I endured. I believed that if I worked harder, or did more for others, I would be worthy of affection. At the end of almost everything, I sacrificed myself, never asserting my boundaries, so I would be liked and earn approval from others. This never earned the desired approval or respect I was seeking.

At some point, I was hoping some knight would come save me, and sweep me off my feet, and that would be my happily ever after. Yet, most had some inner anger, need to control, possessiveness, or an insecurity that was perpetrated, gaslit or they projected, and perpetrated abuse onto me. I found myself tirelessly turning down the interest, in turn, I was scrutinized by an old friend who thought I "just couldn't settle down."

So, I settled, and I ended up in a whirl wind marriage that became abusive. That core need within me to help others, made me susceptible to forget the needs of myself, and prioritize his needs, and his needs alone. I became wrapped up in fear of his consequences, I was convinced "his whole life would be over", if the world around us found out, his truth.

I became protector of his secret, and ultimately lost who I was. I forgot, I was a feminist; I forgot I was working towards my Bachelors Degree, or that I had become a Notary. While my goals fell by the wayside, I forgot that I was beautiful, worthy of love and protection. I forgot that I was enough, just as I was. I forgot that it was okay to disagree, without it leading to, or fearing abuse.

I was so busy fighting to be perfect and for the perfect day, and pretending that nothing was wrong, that I deeply lost the love I had for myself. In order to cope with the abuse, I began hanging on that last perfect memory. I couldn't comprehend that our relationship had been lost after the first day he assaulted me. My smile was as fake as the makeup I painted on my face; I became so good at it. My friends, couldn't stand by as they watched my self-sabotage.

Grief is a feeling that every single one of us has in common. Grief brings a mixed bag of emotions. Anger, sadness, fear, control, anxiety, and depression. Most people are familiar with the five stages of grief, which outlines the stages and that we will go back and forth between all five of these, at any time. One day I would be in denial, the next isolation, depression, anger, bargaining, but mostly I lived with acceptance of this tormented fate, and I learned how to cope with it.

At the end, I realized he wanted me to sacrifice every ounce of myself, for him. I just wanted to be loved. I learned I would never be enough, to earn his respect. I learned, we had very different definitions of love. If I wanted to stay, I had to accept his terms, and his terms alone. In leaving, I not only had to grieve and endure the betrayal of false friends, and a broken marriage, I had to endure the most intense betrayal this world has to offer, betraying my-self. How was it, that I could love people so much, I would go to the ends of the Earth for them, but I couldn't do it for me?

I have been recovering from subjected apathy over the course of my entire life, so none of it was abnormal to me. To normalize this idea, I truly believe that most of us are. I believe we are all craving the Aloha Spirit, and perhaps, we all need a Heart Chakra reboot. Yet, at the same time, I knew apathy was different from the way in which I operated. I knew to my core that apathy was wrong, and I hoped my empathy, could save the world. I was hoping my love was enough to save his.

How Did You Find Healing?

As a struggling Freshman, I was mentally, emotionally and verbally abused by my mom's boyfriend. He told me often I was worthless and a "posterchild for birth control." Regardless, I would find myself picking daisies on the way to work, and giving them out to people who looked lonely, or sad at the mall. For me, it may have been a sign of love to a fellow brother or sister, or a sign of hope and light in darkness. I know, no one, is truly ever alone, regardless of what our mind believes in time of despair. However, I do believe it is the small glimpses of hope that keep us going. Retrospectively, I realize I began practicing Aloha, from a young age, all along.

One pivotal moment occurred when I was 15, when I got into a Spa Capsule. I had been trading massages since I was five years old with friends. Hands, back, feet... however, this Spa Capsule was a full body wave of water, that massaged you while you were face down. The girl that ran it, made fun of me when I asked her for the deepest pressure at a stature of 100lbs, and every single pay day thereafter.

Working for Souper Salad in the Maine Mall, I made the most beautiful salads for people, while I told them they just had to try it out.

I do know, it's easier to revert to the dark road; addiction, anger/rage, jealousy, fear, pity, depression, anxiety, self-harm, and disassociation from life. That is what a lot of us do in situations that leave us distressed.

In any of these states, it is nearly impossible to be empathetic for another. I did find, that with massage, despair could change for me quite drastically. At a fork in the road, massage brought me to the lighter path, infusing love, light and compassion back into me. It was the one way; I knew how to receive love for myself.

For most of my life I didn't realize that I had the power within me, to know that I was enough. I didn't know that I didn't have to be perfect or fight for the approval of others. I could simply approve of myself, and know deep down, that I was more than enough, for myself. I did however recognize that there were some personality traits that I needed to address, if I wanted to be successful. While I had dreamt of becoming a pilot at night, due to my belief, experience, and understanding of the healing that occurred for me with massage, I chose to attend massage school in 2004. Massage school ended up being the most experience healing I had ever witnessed for myself, and for others. My counter parts found me "Most Inspirational".

Why did massage work so well to heal the discord that I was feeling? Massage infuses compassion, loving energy and induces a meditative state that elicits nonjudgmental introspective work to assist in resolving inner pain and root to our "heart blocks". Not only did this compassion replace the apathy I felt from the abuse, I felt as if it was removed. With a wave of every effleurage, I could feel the toxicity from my circumstance leave my being.

Throughout the duration of massage, the mind heads to a meditative state and takes inventory on the pain, discomfort and the enjoyment it is feeling. When thoughts and feelings arise, the mind has the choice to resolve them, or store them for later. I have found that with over 16 years of massage therapy practice and receiving, I am attentive at working to resolve the dust that is kicked up in every massage. This practice I find extremely productive, efficient and effective, which settles my type A personality.

Not only is meditation a mind and body practice, but massage can also facilitate the mind-body connection, and facilitate a deep meditative state of mind. I have found that there is just as much of a disconnect within a lot of people, as there was within myself. I am most excited when people bridge these mind-body connections on the table. Infusing aloha into others and with regular practice of either meditation or massage myself, my mind is calmed, focused, my energy increases, and tranquility is achieved. Regular massage has increased my resiliency and my adaptability to change and tolerance to the long durations of court distress. Massage and meditation has assisted me in realigning my thoughts so I can evaluate tough situations and take much needed action.

Massage and mediation help to resolve the inner workings of not just the body and mind, but of the heart. Throughout the duration of the experience, you look at everything from a nonjudgement space. With massage, you are infused with love, compassion, care, empathy, and innately energetic healing from the

practitioner. Without receiving regular massage, and feeling the transferred love and compassion, and then returning it for others, I strongly believe I would still be struggling with a very intense block in my heart. Seeing the amazing transformation that can happen for people, is why I value client time, when they are in my room and on my table.

After massage school graduation, I began reading books that successful people wrote about being successful. I believed perhaps they could help me pave the way with hints, tricks, and secrets to the trades. I did find a lot of material that shifted my thinking and reality and set me on the path for my best version of success.

Most people could tell you that reading anything from Keith Harrell, Zig Ziglar, or "Into the Magic Shop: A Neurosurgeon's Quest to Discover the Mysteries of the Brain and the Secrets of the Heart" by Dr. James Doty will change your life, and I would have to agree with them.

Keith Harrell would tell you to always have a super fantastic day, Zig Ziglar would encourage you remove other people's garbage from your mind, and get around to the things you've always wanted to do. Dr. James Doty, would tell you, that you can live the life you dream to live if you imagine it in your mind, but you're not actually living, unless you're leading life, with your heart.

The biggest unresolved heart block I struggled with, is that I realized as a public two-time domestic violence and sexual abuse survivor, my perpetrators would not receive the Justice I felt they should have. This feeling was only exacerbated after being fired from a long time dreamed, Spa Manager position, at a high-end hotel for reporting I was intentionally peeped on in the shower. While there were witnesses of the event, still, I was the one left without a job.

In 2018, I decided to finish my Bachelors Degree in Justice with a Minors in Advocacy and Psychology. I deeply wanted to understand why, jail, just wasn't the answer, and I hoped enlightenment would resolve the pain that was aching within me. Honestly, I thought obtaining "Justice" would make me feel better. Instead, every class, provided insight and clarity into the circumstances, laws, and procedures of the court. Finally, I had been afforded understanding and enlightenment. My favorite Professor, James Davitt Esq., incorporated laughter, and lightened my heart every time his humor caught me off guard.

In September 2018, I had taken an advocacy course and was given an assignment to fix something; anything. I closed my eyes and thought about everything I had been through. My heart exclaimed out loud, to address the injustice after injustice, I myself experienced, and resolve what I desperately wanted to be fixed within the justice system. I realize, you can't address everything at once, however, you can start with step number one.

The question posed out loud to myself was, not: "why didn't she leave", I had a million reasons why I couldn't leave; I'm sure she has them too. The question was "how do I get her out sooner?". The time it takes to find the right numbers, agencies, the time that is spent on the phone is daunting to someone in crisis, as distress overrules cognitive function. This is the leading reason victims of violence should be represented by court appointed attorneys, however, instead of focusing on writing a paper on a balance in court representation for victims of violence in Family Court proceedings, I decided I would write a paper about creating an app, that would consolidate crisis response services into one platform to provide ease, efficiency, and effectiveness for recovering victims of traumatic environments.

Then, I thought, it may be better if I had a prototype to accompany my paper.

I started with step one. I found an app generator that really didn't work the way I had anticipated, so I tried another. This one, seemed to allow me to work within the click funnel actions I had hoped for, and I had envisioned in my mind. I sat on my bed, for three days straight, I did not shower, and I ate all my meals in bed. The click funnel was working, my prototype was coming alive, I just couldn't stop. I thought, if this app helps one person, it would be amazing and serve its purpose. I believe I got an A+ on the assignment, as excited as I was about that, I began reaching out to see if anyone would be interested in taking the idea. I had people that seemed interested in how it was put together, I didn't have anyone interested in taking it on as a project. So, eight months later, after walking with the rest of the UMA Justice Class of 2019, I became a Notary once again, and I Founded a Nonprofit called Safe House, in the state of Maine.

From there, I recruited a team of survivors to assist me in a project to take on the National Expansion of the Safe House Crisis App, and then the mirrored Safe House Recovery App, that we led solely, with our hearts. With every new agency entry, we know that we will be reaching at least one more person. What is built every day with this team, the growth, the change, the love, the inspiration is unlike anything I have ever been a part of. We have found each other, after the darkest hell, and we are working together on something far larger than ourselves, championing justice, by becoming the beacon of light to those in darkness looking for a safer place, sooner.

Now, I hadn't imagined Safe House would have assisted me in resolving the hurt I felt and feel within me. The collaboration on Safe House projects assists me in opening my heart towards others and progresses my life toward who I am today. Now, instead ruminating and stunting my life by allowing those left behind looking to paint me in a negative light, I'm no longer spending my time struggling to refute it. I began to live a productive life, and therefore halted the ill, contagious, rumored, and destructive conversations that were happening backstage, almost completely.

In August of 2019, I still dreamt I would open a Hawai'ian themed spa, where I could assist people to get to a better place within their body, mind, spirit, and within their heart. I wanted to take people on their guided mediation. I took the place that I imagined in my mind for decades, turned it a reality, and created an ultimate healing destination. Spa Voyage is a place where people could find a safe container to immerse their senses into a tropical vibe, receive aloha, and effectively, hang loose.

To pull this off correctly, I knew I needed to understand the culture and the environment for myself. So, I traveled to Hawai'i, and fully immersed myself in the environment. I hung out with locals, went hula dancing, surfed with a sea turtle, engaged in making and wearing leis, hiked and snorkeled Hanauma bay, I meditated with lava rock, through a lava tube, ate the most incredible food, listened to music, and felt all the aloha spirt that surrounded me. I found my aloha moment.

When I got home, something happened I didn't expect. I had always known I wanted to create this Hawai'ian getaway for Mainers, what I didn't realize, was just how bad I felt it needed to be done. When I got back from Hawai'i, the feeling within me to share the aloha spirit called as a necessity. Today, up and running, I continue to hope my tropical staycation assists those looking for some seasonal affective relief, as well as an implied transformative meditation, coupled with massage and spa service for the ultimate heart healing, and truly a tranquil experience.

There is only one piece left to my puzzle I have been working on picking up, and that is my secret dream to become a commercial pilot. As a child, I would look up at the stars and watch the airliners shoot across the sky, and like most aviators I would wish on them like shooting stars. The feeling of staring off and reaching for the infinite night, brought me solace as a kid and throughout my years. It wasn't until 2017 at a hotel in New Hampshire, that I met a 99 (Women Pilot), in a breakfast line that I was told, "you can do it".

I do realize there are so many limitations within our minds that prevent us from becoming who we wish to become. We need to believe we can do, anything we want to do. We need to make the plan and execute the plan. I needed to make the plan, and then execute the plan. While the steps did seem somewhat daunting, I started again, with step one.

I joined Women in Aviation, and became an active member in a local chapter, I began associating with the most inspirational and tenacious, women leaders of aviation and aerospace. I then, was selected to attend the most amazing Women in Aviation Conference, I was inspired at the WAI Conference to reach for the stars, obtain my Student Pilot's License, and then join the 99s.

One step, and day at a time, we paint the walls of our reality. Every day of my life, I believe I can soar and reach the heights of my heart, the only limitations, are in my mind. Flying through air, elates my heart and opens my mind, that anything we dream we can do; we can do. I'm sure the Wright Brothers, Sally Ride, and Amelia Earhart felt it. It took a long time for me to learn the domestic violence I endured, was not a limitation within my heart, but that it was some sort of limitation and much needed healing within the perpetrator's.

How Could Others Find Healing?

In mediation and massage, you can envision anywhere in the world, you want to go. You can head to Hawai'i in your mind, just by imagining that you feel the warmth on your skin and the sand under your feet. You can smell the fragrant plumeria flowers and feel the wind on your face as it blows by. You can paint your life, and your environment any way you want to, every single day. Once you begin to envision a better life, you realize that you overseeing change, and then living it.

With meditation and massage neuroplasticity can occur, you can rewire your synapse, and change your mind in every session. In these two healing modalities, you are dancing between alpha and theta waves, these two waves occur between relaxing, meditation and daydreaming. They calm your body, mind, slow the heart rate, blood pressure, muscle tension, and allow you center in your own personal well-being, providing tranquility, and over time enhancing your quality of life. With practice some people learn the ability control their own brain waves and find themselves entering the delta brain waves, found in our dreamless sleep, which initiate healing and resets our internal clock. With practice, maybe you can be in charge of this type of healing too.

Case studies have shown that just listening to relaxing music for 30 minutes, is similar to taking 10mg of Valium. With this in mind, if you went into a spa and received a 90-minute massage, that relaxing music in the background would equate to about 30mg of Valium. Which is in addition to the natural high felt during massage and mediation as in a combined effort promotes a release of endorphins, which also assists in decreasing anxiety, stress hormone, muscle tension, depression, relieving rumination and fear, and bringing us toward self- actualization.

If you are interested in looking to incorporate Reiki healing into your life to assist you with some Heart Chakra blockages, there are a couple of ways you can do this. One of the first ways, is finding a Reiki provider, and experience a Reiki healing session that is customized to balance your energetic needs. Another way of approaching Reiki is finding a Reiki Master, who can teach you a Level One Reiki Course, which will provide you with the tools to balance your 7 Chakras, including the Heart Chakra, by yourself.

If I were to create a road map from some of the healing work, I have done myself it would look something like this:

- Start loving yourself. When it seems like you can't love yourself. Start looking at yourself, through the eyes of loved ones.
- Fill your cup first. Someone might not go out of their way for you, you must go out of your way for yourself. Some people are still learning to be the hero of their own story, they may not be able to be the hero of yours.
- Set boundaries. It's okay to not take a call, turn off your phone, not go out to dinner, make new friends, or say I cannot talk about this right now.
- Be Early. Being early, means you show up for yourself. You're ahead of the game.
- Don't internalize the actions of others, what is going on with them, is going on with them.
- Stay positive. There is a silver lining in everything if you look close enough. Everything does, happen for a reason. Trust the closed doors.

- Celebration. Surround yourself with people that celebrate you, and let go those who don't.
- Replenish Right. Schedule breaks and replenish your body with feel good food and a healthy water intake. If you feel like garbage after you eat something, don't eat it.
- Live. Imagine your day is a blank sheet of white paper. What will you do with it? You can paint whatever picture you want. If there is something you don't like, change it.
- Learn your patterns. Start assessing your behaviors, take inventory. Good, bad, and indifferent. Start working on strengthening your traits, one day, and moment at a time.
- SPA. Massage, body treatments, reiki, and acupuncture, are among the most healing modalities in this world. Releasing restrictions in the body and in your heart will help you be the best person you can be.
- Travel. Save your money, find ways to travel, and check Hawaii off your bucket list. Hawai'i, is the one place were the Heart Chakra/ Aloha Spirit is alive and well.
- Voyage. Live everyday as if you are on vacation. Imagine every day you are waking up, headed to the nearest airport, with your best clothes. Notice the person that emerges, when you're on vacation, and harness that person, in your everyday life.
- Forgive and show grace. As you would want others to forgive you. Moving forward can move mountains, releasing your heart.
- Just be; and be easy on yourself. Gears switch after you obtain perfection. You will always be in the mode of obtaining perfection with a narcissist. Don't be narcissistic with yourself or expect more from yourself, than you would others.
- Reach out if you need help and leave early if you see red flags or toxic patterns and behaviors.

- Emotions are waves, they ebb and flow. Ride the wave, don't let them consume you.
- Upstanding. Be the one to stand up, even when everything is on the line.
- Validate and Normalize. If you can do these two things with any problem you have, is it truly as big as it seems?
- Community and leadership. Join a nonprofit whose heart and mission is aligned with yours, and become part of the effort to initiate the changes you would like to see in the world.
- Greet and help everyone you meet, with Aloha.
- Have FUN! Live life through a child-like lens. Love others as if your heart is unbreakable, and live like your heart has never been broken.

Life experiences can be amazing, or traumatic. The key to living the best life possible, it not to let others with heart blocks, turn your heart against yourself, or others. It is with life's crazy and hurtful experiences that something profound is happening within you. With each situation in which you choose empathy over apathy, that rock situated in between your chest, is pressurized into the diamond it is meant to be. The truth is we can begin to uncover the dimensions of our diamond hearts, whenever we want to.

ELIZA CONLEY-LEPENE

My name is Eliza Conley-Lepene, I am the Owner of Eliza LLC, Spa Voyage, Founder of Safe House (YourSaferPlace.org), and the Creator of the Safe House Crisis and Recovery Apps, President of Women in Aviation Connecticut Chapter. I have a Bachelors Degree in Justice with Minors in Advocacy and Psychology.

Alongside being a Massage Therapist, I have engaged in lifelong healing practices which have included but have not been limited to Spa Services, Mediation, Dance Therapy, and Reiki. I obtained a Certification in Energy Medicine from the Hawai'i Community, in order to provide direction, explanation, and clarity to those looking for healing, and energetic understanding of oneself.

CHAPTER 20

Vicarious Trauma

Emily Singerhouse

My name is Emily Singerhouse. I am a researcher, educator, and lifelong student. I came from a very small town in Northwestern Wisconsin. The image people have of Wisconsin is very accurate to what might be imagined about my hometown. There was farmland, cows, bars, a river that ran through the downtown, and of course, more farmland. I grew up in a modest home in the middle of the woods alongside my sister and parents. At a very young age, I knew that I wanted more out of life than what my town of 1,000 people had to offer. I wanted to go to college to become a marine biologist, live in Australia, travel around Europe, get married, and so much more. My young mind's imagination had no limits. Although, my vision for the future blanketed my conception of daily life.

What I didn't realize was that I was undergoing Adverse Childhood Experiences (ACES). ACES are traumatic events that happen during childhood. For example, experiencing violence or growing up in a home with substance abuse issues are two of the many traumatic experiences for children. For me, I experienced many different things, but the one that was the most pronounced was growing up with a parent with addiction. I felt neglected, unable to understand what normalcy was, and had severe trust issues. I blamed myself for their substance abuse addiction. I was not shown what a healthy adult relationship looked like. To me, it was yelling, secrets, and control. At 14, my parents got a divorce. I felt a weight come off my shoulders. Like most kids in my hometown, I tried to cure the pain of what continued on at home with substance use and rebellion. I was being bullied at school and I felt angry and alone in the world. To me, using substances was a way to be with others. I longed for friendship, but didn't know how to have friends. I wanted a relationship, but didn't know how to express love. Being rebellious got me attention; but really I was crying out for help. I was convinced into thinking that was part of my personality traits. No one ever asked me what was happening or if I was okay. Now that I am older, I wish someone did.

To this day, I am still trying to figure out how to have a healthy relationship with myself and the people I love. Though I experienced multiple adversities growing up, I am learning to overcome them. I became a first generation college graduate- twice. I started my own independent consulting business. Now, I am on my way to becoming published in multiple academic journals, present at conferences internationally, and continue to dive deeper into my work. I have learned the pain of asking for help, and being vulnerable with myself. I have learned to heal with my trauma and accept myself for everything that I am. I have understood my heart block.

To continue into a little deeper of who I am, I am a community-based participatory action researcher. In other words, I conduct qualitative research hand and hand with community members. My work has focused on the issues of human trafficking, sexual violence, domestic violence, youth exploitation, and community wellbeing. I specialized in pattern and anomaly identification of human trafficking operations, prevention of sexual and domestic violence, and holistic wellness enhancement for communities. Something that I have learned over the last few years is how each facet in our society plays into the reasons why people experience violence. Whether it's the food we eat, the media we consume, or the politics happening across the world; it is all connected. That is in part why I do the work that I do. I believe that collectively, we can help change the ways that we prevent, intervene, and empower our communities to be free from violence. My current mission is to provide research and communication to organizations working on the issues of human trafficking, sexual violence, domestic violence, and community wellbeing. I have, and will continue to, dedicate my life to this movement.

PART II (My experience)

Usually when people hear the term vicarious trauma, they don't know what it is. To define vicarious trauma, it is the result of a traumatic experience from working with survivors of trauma and violence. Personally, I prefer to call it "second-hand trauma," but for the purpose of this chapter, vicarious trauma is the terminology I will use. I personally experienced vicarious trauma through working directly with, listening to transcripts, and reviewing case files of survivors of human trafficking and sexual violence. I remember the first time I read a transcription of an interview with a survivor of commercial sexual exploitation. I was an unpaid intern looking to help on a project that was to understand services that should be offered to survivors. I read about brutal sexual assault stories, mistreatment by healthcare systems and abuse from law enforcement. I was very emotional. For a moment, I thought maybe I should step away from this. But after I read the horrors, there was no way I would be able to turn back from this and continue down my path of ignorance. Once someone gets exposed to the darkness of the clandestine, underground market of commercial sexual exploitation, you can never forget. I realized during this first project that this work is not for the faint of heart.

I continued on. After a few years, I became a full-time employee of the University of Minnesota. I got to the point where I had the security clearance to view, code, and analyze private law enforcement case files. Those case files contain violent experiences that I wouldn't wish upon my worst enemy. I became engulfed in them. As a researcher, there was so much rich data to understand. I spent over 250 hours analyzing and coding case files. I internalized the traumatic moments and began to ruminate on even the smaller details of my case files. For example, when I noticed a victim's birthday was around the time I was reading the documents, and I found myself questioning what she may have been doing on her birthday; if she was even still alive. I later found out she wasn't.

I remember reading about a very graphic sexual assault of a child that completely gripped my perception of life. I was working from my home in Minneapolis due to the COVID-19 pandemic. I was shaking, tears rolling down my face, and wincing as I continued through the transcript from this child. I was thinking to myself, "Why? Why must people do such cruel things to young children? Is there any humanity left in this world?" I was never the same after this. I had difficulty sleeping. I would have nightmares of being trafficked and seeing what I imagined the children looked like. I wondered where they were. I felt disbelief, had little faith in humanity, and wanted to end my research career. I was in doubt that these issues could ever be solved. I bear witness to survivors recounting their violent experiences, their lives, and how they had to overcome what happened to them. I had heard and seen too much pain and suffering, while also dealing with my own trauma. Later, I came to understand the vicarious trauma that comes from engulfung oneself in such raw material can feel a change in world view, compelled to do the work, satisfaction with their lives, or feel nothing at all. For me, I had a complete change in world view and burned out until I started to take the steps to heal from these experiences.

PART III (The brain, body, and trauma)

Many people experience mental and physical health impacts during a traumatic episode. Most of the time, people don't know why that happens. I take on a trauma-informed approach when working on the issues of human trafficking and violence; however, I am not a neuroscientist or a healthcare worker. I am an experienced trauma professional and educator on issues relating to violence. As part of understanding my own trauma and to help others do the same, I have done research on understanding what happens to the body and brain during a traumatic experience.

When we experience trauma, the brain undergoes neurological changes which are connected to physiological regulation. The effects of trauma on the brain can manifest as uncontrollable emotional regulation, constant states of hyper/hypovigilance, memory loss, toxic stress, and more. The areas of the brain primarily responsible for the results of trauma are the hippocampus, amygdala, and prefrontal cortex. These parts of the brain are involved in the explicit and implicit memory. Regarding trauma, the explicit memory affects the episodic memory, where events and experiences are stored. The implicit memory is affected by the emotional memory attached to the trauma. The roles of the hippocampus, amygdala, and prefrontal cortex in the memory process are encoding, storing, and recalling. The storage part of the memory process, controlled by the hippocampus, is a very fragile stage of the process. When an experience is highly intense and emotional, it can shut down and fragment the events stored as the episodic memory. Additionally, the amygdala has a role in the implicit memory, or the parts of the brain that controls the emotional memory. The amygdala responds to past sensory experiences. Traumatic memories are archived in a way that "marks" future situations as threatening or stressful to protect them from future trauma. The amygdala goes into overdrive, and it is almost uncontrollable until addressed. A study showed that people who are diagnosed with post-traumatic stress disorder (PTSD) have highly reactive brains. This study showed that PTSD patients have severe neurological differences compared to patients without PTSD.Results of the brain being disturbed by trauma experiences can sometimes result in mental health diagnoses such as PTSD, depression, anxiety, and more. Emotions such as agitation, numbness, spouts of anger, confusion, difficulty concentrating, guilt, fear, shock, unawareness of danger, and more can also be present.

As stated, the body is deeply connected to the brain in its response to traumatic experience. Due to the psychological impact of trauma, the body is left with an imprint which can become severe if left untreated and unprocessed. A study found that patients with PTSD have poorer physical health ranging from cardiovascular, gastrointestinal, immunological, and more. Although, it is important to note that the severity of the physical impacts of trauma are dependent on the severity of the episode, socio-economic status, biological sex, substance use, and more. Regardless, physical impacts are still a result of trauma. I believe that during traumatic episodes, we tense up and store stress in different parts of our body. For me, I had constant pain in my upper left shoulder after experiencing trauma. Even going to the chiropractor didn't help. It wasn't until I started going to therapy that the physical pain started to alleviate. Many people who experience trauma report having chronic pain, migraines, pelvic pain, muscle pain, problems with their immune system, and more.

For people who have experienced vicarious trauma, the brain and body are affected in very fascinating ways. Since the physical experience didn't happen directly to that person, it is almost entirely a mentally stimulating experience. People working in law enforcement, emergency medical treatment, and victim services are repeatedly exposed to trauma, which creates a toxic stress response in their brains. One could say their emotional memory is the most affected by their vicarious trauma experience. They empathize deeply with the survivor, are overwhelmed by what they saw or heard, and can sometimes lose control. For vicarious trauma survivors, they can also suffer from mental health diagnosis, such as PTSD. Results from vicarious trauma can be negative, neutral, or positive. Figure 1 outlines the spectrum of responses felt by work-related exposure to trauma.

Burnout is a very common result among people who have vicarious trauma. This experience is something that can be felt both physically and mentally. People have reported feeling sleepiness, fatigue, easily distracted, aches, and more. Physically, vicarious trauma survivors are affected during their day to day activities. This can affect their performance, morale, relationships, and behavior. Personally, I felt easily distracted from my work, avoiding tasks, starting work later than usual, and had poorer performance.

PART IV (Healing & overcoming vicarious trauma)

Overcoming my heart block has been a multiple years long process. It was never a straight line, and I fell off multiple times. I used to live in a haze of just experiencing things and then moving on. I rarely looked internally; I mean really looked. I could say that I was mindful, but that was putting a bandage over my past to have a better outward impression of myself for others. The future was never something I planned or looked forward to, and I definitely was not reflecting on the past. I chose ignorance over reality which eventually led me to mentally hit rock bottom. To get to the point of healing and thriving, I attended therapy, spent time in nature, leaned on my family and friends, and spent a lot of time getting creative with painting. I had to open myself up to what

I experienced. Today, I have learned how to hear traumatic experiences with acceptance of reality and the determination to continue. I had to look internally to understand why I internalized and empathized so much with these experiences of survivors. I had to learn how my body and brain responded to trauma to truly understand how to heal. I have learned what resilience means to me. To me, resiliency is taking time for myself, expressing emotions, having boundaries, and the passion to continue.

For vicarious trauma survivors, it is crucial to have a workplace that understands and is supportive of these experiences. Vicarious trauma-informed organizations can proactively respond to and address the impacts of trauma for their employees. Something that I learned coming from an academic background was to reach out to co-workers on an individual level to talk about how their work might be affecting them. Holding space for open dialog and emotional regulation is critical in having a functional team that addresses vicarious trauma. Healing from trauma is not an easy feat. It requires effort every single day. Healing does not have a step by step solution. Here are some recommendations for taking the steps to heal:

Seek therapy to process the experiences and emotions. Some options for therapy are EMDR, DBT, Group and behavior therapy

Exercise to get the body moving in ways that feel good. This can help reconnect with yourself

Spend time in nature. This can bring a new sense of connection, power, and self-reflection

Lean on family and friends. Opening up with others about how you are feeling is important to avoid isolation and loneliness.

Get into a routine. This can help create a healthy work-life balance, find places to grow, and re-establish yourself.

Attend celebrations, events, and activities that you are passionate about. Sometimes taking the step to reconnect with something you like to do is a good step to get back to your own normalcy.

Take some time with the arts. Listening to music, meditation, and harvesting your creativity can be good ways to express yourself when you are having a hard time.

Conclusion

Vicarious trauma is an experience that is widespread and affects many people every day. Results of trauma within the brain and body are distinctly connected. Together, they create a response that changes neurological and physiological composition that affects our day to day lives. I had to learn the hard way what I was experiencing before being educated on vicarious trauma and how humans naturally react to it. Something that I have taken away after overcoming my heart block was the power of moving forward. I learned how much better life is once I took that step. I was more passionate about my work, family, friends, and most importantly, myself. Reconnecting after understanding how my trauma was blocking me from reaching my full potential was one of the most inspiring experiences. I can look at myself and see night and day from the person I was before. After overcoming my heart block, I have found a new life.

EMILY SINGERHOUSE

Emily Singerhouse is the founder of Singerhouse Research Consulting LLC, qualitative researcher by training, advocate and educator on the issues of human trafficking, domestic violence, sexual violence, youth exploitation, racial equality, and community wellbeing. I have worked on trans-disciplinary teams ranging from academics, to survivors, to law enforcement. I have researched human trafficking network structures, network recruitment, network disruptions, illicit activity, youth trading sex, systemic response to sexual violence, virtual engagement of exploited youth, and so much more. Currently, I am studying quantitative research methods to perfect mixed-methods research. I am a part of academic publications, conference presentations, state-wide webinars, trainings, and more. I am looking to leverage community partnerships to dig-deeper into stigmatized issues affecting our society today.

https://www.singerhouseresearch.com/

REFERENCES

1 Centers for Disease Control and Prevention (2021) Preventing Adverse Childhood Experiences. https://www.cdc.gov/violenceprevention/aces/fastfact.html?CDC_AA_refVal=https%3A%2F%2Fwww.cdc.gov%2Fviolenceprevention%2Facestudy%2Ffastfact.html

2 Office for Victims in Crime (2016) What is Vicarious Trauma. https://ovc.ojp.gov/program/vtt/what-is-vicarious-trauma#what-is-vicarious-trauma

3 Office for Victims of Crime (n.d) The Vicarious Trauma Toolkit: What is Vicarious Trauma? Office for Victims of Crime. https://ovc.ojp.gov/program/vtt/what-is-vicarious-trauma#what-is-vicarious-trauma

4 Treatment Improvement Protocol (TIP) Series, No. 57. Center for Substance Abuse Treatment (US). Rockville (MD): Substance Abuse and Mental Health Services Administration (US); 2014.

5 The National Institute for the Clinical Application of Behavioral Medicine (2017). https://www.naadac.org/assets/2416/2019NWRC_Michael_Bricker_Handout4.pdf

6 Mayfield Brain & Spin (2019

7 Esterlis, Irina (n.d). https://news.yale.edu/2017/07/17/new-ptsd-study-identifies-potential-path-treatment

8 Treatment Improvement Protocol (TIP) (2014) Series, No. 57. Center for Substance Abuse Treatment (US). Rockville (MD): Substance Abuse and Mental Health Services Administration (US).

9 Treatment Improvement Protocol (TIP) (2014) Series, No. 57. Center for Substance Abuse Treatment (US). Rockville (MD): Substance Abuse and Mental Health Services Administration (US).

10 Stam, Rianne (2006). PTSD and stress sensitisation: A tale of brain and body Part 1: Human studies. Neuroscience and Biobehavioral Review.

11 Lesser, Ben. (2021). How Trauma Affects the Human Body. Dual Diagnosis. https://dualdiagnosis.org/mental-health-and-addiction/post-traumatic-stress-disorder-and-addiction/how-trauma-affects-the-human-body/

12 Northeastern Universities Urban Health Research and Practice (2013). Introduction to Vicarious Trauma for Victims Services. Office for Victims of Crime.

13 Northeastern Universities Urban Health Research and Practice (2013). Introduction to Vicarious Trauma for Victims Services. Office for Victims of Crime.

How the Heart Works;

"Your heart's electrical system controls the rate and rhythm of your heartbeat": https://www.nhlbi.nih.gov/health-topics/how-heart-works#:~:text=Your%20heart%20has%20a%20special,the%20heart%20to%20the%20bottom.&text=The%20ventricles%20relax%2C%20and%20the,again%20in%20the%20SA%20node

Heart Rhythm Versus Conduction;

"In cases of heart block, the electrical signals that progress from the heart's upper chambers (atria) to its lower chambers (ventricles) are impaired. When those signals don't transmit properly, the heart beats irregularly." https://www.heart.org/en/health-topics/arrhythmia/about-arrhythmia/conduction-disorders

Heart block Defined:

1. https://medlineplus.gov/ency/article/007658.htm
2. https://my.clevelandclinic.org/health/diseases/17056-heart-block#:~:text=Heart%20block%2C%20also%20called%20AV,tiredne%20ss%20and%20shortness%20of%20breath

Electrical System of the Heart;

"What makes your heart rate speed up or slow down"
https://www.mottchildren.org/health-library/te7147abc

Trauma-Induced Conduction Disturbances (2018 Case):
https://www.ncbi.nlm.nih.gov/pmc/articles/PMC6162130/

CPSIA information can be obtained
at www.ICGtesting.com
Printed in the USA
LVHW061635021221
704815LV00001BA/60